# Incidental Exposure to Online News

# Synthesis Lectures on Information Concepts, Retrieval, and Services

Editor

**Gary Marchionini**, *University of North Carolina, Chapel Hill*

Synthesis Lectures on Information Concepts, Retrieval, and Services publishes short books on topics pertaining to information science and applications of technology to information discovery, production, distribution, and management. Potential topics include: data models, indexing theory and algorithms, classification, information architecture, information economics, privacy and identity, scholarly communication, bibliometrics and webometrics, personal information management, human information behavior, digital libraries, archives and preservation, cultural informatics, information retrieval evaluation, data fusion, relevance feedback, recommendation systems, question answering, natural language processing for retrieval, text summarization, multimedia retrieval, multilingual retrieval, and exploratory search.

viii

Incidental Exposure to Online News
Borchuluun Yadamsuren and Sanda Erdelez


ISBN: 978-3-031-01177-1    print
ISBN: 978-3-031-02305-7    ebook

DOI 10.1007/978-3-031-02305-7

A Publication in the Springer series
*SYNTHESIS LECTURES ON INFORMATION CONCEPTS, RETRIEVAL, AND SERVICES #54*
Series Editor: Gary Marchionini, University of North Carolina, Chapel Hill

Series ISSN 1947-945X  Print    1947-9468  Electronic

# Incidental Exposure to Online News

Borchuluun Yadamsuren
Columbia College, Columbia, Missouri

Sanda Erdelez
School of Information Science and Learning Technologies
University of Missouri, Columbia, Missouri

*SYNTHESIS LECTURES ON INFORMATION CONCEPTS,
RETRIEVAL, AND SERVICES #54*

## ABSTRACT

Rapid technological changes and availability of news anywhere and at any moment have changed how people seek out news. Increasingly, consumers no longer take deliberate actions to read the news, instead stumbling upon news online. While the emergence of serendipitous news discovery online has been recognized in the literature, there is a limited understanding about how people experience this behavior. Based on the mixed method study that investigated online news reading behavior of residents in a Midwestern U.S. town, we explore how people accidentally discover news when engaged in various online activities. Employing the grounded theory approach, we define Incidental Exposure to Online News (IEON) as individual's memorable experiences of chance encounters with interesting, useful, or surprising news while using the Internet for news browsing or for non-news-related online activities, such as checking email or visiting social networking sites. The book presents a conceptual framework of IEON that advances research and an understanding of serendipitous news discovery from people's holistic experiences of news consumption in their everyday lives. The proposed IEON Process Model identifies key steps in an IEON experience that could help news reporters and developers of online news platforms create innovative storytelling and design strategies to catch consumers' attention during their online activities. Finally, this book raises important methodological questions for further investigation: how should serendipitous news discovery be studied, measured, and observed, and what are the essential elements that differentiate this behavior from other types of online news consumption and information behaviors?

## KEYWORDS

incidental exposure to news, serendipitous news discovery, information encountering, news encountering, serendipity, online news, news consumption, news reading behavior

*Dedicated to our parents and families*

# Contents

# Preface

*The function of news is to orient man and society in an actual world* (Park, 1940).

The impetus for this book started when Dr. Borchuluun Yadamsuren (the first author) became fascinated with the concept of *information encountering* (IE) while taking a seminar by Dr. Sanda Erdelez (the co-author) entitled Human Information Behavior, at the School of Information Science and Learning Technologies at the University of Missouri. Later, Dr. Yadamsuren came across an article on incidental exposure to news in *Journalism and Mass Communication Quarterly*. This experience sparked the idea to conduct her dissertation research on the interesting and emerging topic of serendipity and online news consumption, applying IE, as a conceptual framework.

This book presents outcomes of an ongoing, multiyear research program, the scope of which reaches far beyond a dissertation study alone. Numerous discussions about incidental exposure to news with scholars in information science and mass communication as well as everyday people, online news consumers, have helped us rethink and rediscover different dimensions of the collected data. Two quantifications of the process of re-analysis included returning to over 300 pages of interview transcripts and multiple replays of close to 25 hours of recorded sessions.

This process has continually reinforced the complexity of the research topic. Chief among the many challenges associated with this complexity has been the pursuit of understanding on two phenomena that are fast developing and (almost) impossible to catch up with: news and technology. As Park (1940) wrote, news itself is a "very perishable commodity."

*News remains news only when it has reached the persons for whom it has "news interest." Once published and its significance recognized, what was news becomes history. This transient and ephemeral quality is of the very essence of news and is intimately connected with every other character that it exhibits. Different types of news have a different time span. In its most elementary form a news report is a mere "flash," announcing that an event has happened. If the event proves of real importance, interest in it will lead to further inquiry and to a more complete acquaintance with the attendant circumstances. An event ceases to be news, however, as soon as the tension it aroused has ceased and public attention has been directed to some other*

*aspect of the habitat or to some other incident sufficiently novel, exciting, or import-*
*ant to hold its attention* (p. 670).

In this sense, we grappled with the "transient and ephemeral" nature of news in our investigation of serendipitous news discovery. Many news stories reported by our respondents as a part of their incidental exposure to online news (IEON) experience are already historical references, flash announcements of certain important events during the time of data collection and interview sessions. Still, we believe that those news stories, historical as they inherently and inevitably become, could enrich our understanding of the principles of IEON behavior when we direct our attention to the nature of a news story, the event covered in it, and the attention-grabbing elements that led readers to incidental exposure.

The second challenge in our investigation of IEON was the ever-changing technologies for both news delivery and news consumption. The study presented here reflects IEON and online news consumption behavior involving the technologies available during the data collection period, which was prior to the recent explosion in the use of tablets and other smart devices. However, we argue that the general patterns of behaviors identified in the IEON process model, as presented in this book, are independent of the types of mobile digital devices. While specific strategies and tools to capture, share, and save the encountered news stories could be different based on the specific device in use, the main focus is on identifying the IEON and its process steps to inform the development of innovative tools that enable news consumers to benefit from serendipitous news discovery.

Finally, this book is an attempt to present a conceptual framework that identifies and investigates IEON based on study data that captured only a slice of everyday online news consumption and the IEON experiences of residents in an American Midwestern college town. Such slices will undoubtedly differ by community, culture, and country, depending on numerous factors, such as lifestyle, media system, technology penetration, and so on. We leave the exploration of this territory for future research.

# Acknowledgments

The authors are indebted to Dr. John Budd for his insightful suggestions in the early stages of this research, Dr. Linda Steiner for her thoughtful comments and suggestions on the first draft of the manuscript, and Dr. Marta Ferguson for her editorial help. This lecture would not have been published without the support of Dr. Gary Marchionini and Diane Cerra, who coordinated all important work related to the publishing process.

Borchuluun Yadamsuren is indebted to her family for their continuous support and unconditional love and especially to her husband Jagdagdorj Erkhembayar for encouragement to complete this book. She is most grateful to her daughter, Nomin-Erdene Jagdagdorj for her meticulous editing on the early drafts of this manuscript and for the graphic design of the two models presented in this book: the IEON conceptual framework and the IEON process model. She is also grateful to Dr. Esther Thorson for her encouragement to apply IEON in a social game context and to the Reynolds Journalism Institute at the University of Missouri for supporting the development of this application.

Sanda Erdelez is grateful to the University of Missouri Mizzou Advantage strategic initiative for awarding two grants to her research group on Opportunistic Discovery of Information. These grants provided funding for her ongoing research on IE and also supported the research activities presented in this book. She is thankful to her daughter Eva Petakovic for providing editorial help and also grateful to her numerous students and colleagues from all around the world for promoting interest in the role of serendipity in human information behavior.

CHAPTER 1

# Introduction

## 1.1 OVERVIEW

The Internet and mobile technologies are rapidly changing news consumption, offering consumers both minute-by-minute updates on developing stories and more freedom to choose news from different locations at their convenience. The increased reliance on online news consumption stimulates ongoing discussion among communication scholars on how the Internet may either contribute or be harmful to maintaining an active citizenry for a democratic society (Dahl, 1989; Delli Carpini, and Keeter, 1996).

The optimistic views in this discussion revolve around the prospects of the Internet to broaden the public sphere (Habermas, 1989) with virtual places, such as comment fields, live blogs, social media, and news sites. This is an area where a range of ideas concerning public affairs could be exchanged in a way that is more free from the constraints of individual status and identity. The Internet provides citizens with easy access to ample information about politics and news and, as such, has the potential to contribute to a healthy democracy. The pessimistic view in this discussion centers on people's increased capacity to customize their own selection of news, allowing them to avoid important information on public affairs and turning them into "information hermits" (Trilling and Schoenbach, 2012) who pick only the news that fits their narrow interest. In addition, various algorithmic personalization filters provided by Internet search engines bring the danger of so-called filter bubbles (Pariser, 2011) or "echo chambers" that prevent individuals from engaging with ideas different from their own (Sunstein, 2001).

Serendipitous exposure to online news has emerged as a potential solution for escaping the invisible barriers that prevent access to diversified information. Tewksbury et al. (2001) were the first to point out that the prevalence of news on the web provides opportunities for people to encounter news when not expected, as a by-product of other online activities. They identified this type of behavior as "incidental exposure to news" and defined it as "encountering current affairs knowledge while performing some other task" (p. 538). Zuckerman (2013) recognized a need to "engineer serendipity" to break small circles of communication, or "digital flocks," and to rewire the Internet so that people will have more opportunities to avoid digital self-segregation.

He argued that expanded opportunities for serendipitous news exposure may help people overcome the perils of news filter bubbles and audience fragmentation.

Despite the conceptual recognition of serendipitous discovery of online news in mass communication literature, this topic has received limited systematic research attention. The literature provides inconsistent terms for this type of behavior: incidental online news exposure (Tewksbury et al., 2001), serendipitous news consumption (Purcell et al., 2010), stumbling upon news on the Internet, unintentional news exposure, accidental news exposure (Kim et al., 2013), and simply—serendipity (Salwen et al., 2005).

The study presented in this book was motivated by the need for a comprehensive understanding about the concept of serendipity in online news consumption and questions about its broader impact. How do people experience incidental exposure to online news (IEON)? Do these experiences promote the citizens' fortuitous discovery of crosscutting information and produce the positive outcomes envisioned by Mutz (2006) and Zuckerman (2013)? The research reported here explores how people serendipitously experience online news by taking into account behavioral, cognitive, and affective aspects of this phenomenon. It was inspired by the literature on mass media consumption and human information behavior within library and information science (LIS) research.

The theoretical frameworks and accompanying methodological approaches in LIS studies of serendipity in information seeking provided the initial steps to study serendipitous news discovery in depth. A central argument of this research posits that people with distinct behavioral, cognitive, and affective characteristics experience serendipitous news discovery while engaged in various online activities that are related to their information needs in what Savolainen (1995) identified as Everyday Life Information Seeking (ELIS) contexts. The ELIS model states that information source preferences and use patterns are socially conditioned, despite the fact that individuals select and use various sources to solve problems or make sense of their everyday world.

Serendipity in information behavior emerged as a research topic in the field of information science in the mid-1990s through the work of Dr. Erdelez (1997). She labeled this behavior as information encountering (IE), meaning "memorable experiences of accidental discovery of useful and interesting information" (p. 412). Erdelez developed a conceptual framework to study IE. The four dimensions of Erdelez's (2000) IE model were as follows: the information user (who encountered information), the environment (setting in which information was encountered), the information (what was encountered), and the information need (the need that was addressed with encountered information). Erdelez (2000) described IE as "an incident or event that usually intersects with some other information acquisition-related activity such as information seeking and browsing." This theoretical framework and accompanying methodology provide guidance in the investigation of serendipitous news discovery.

Our study employs a constructivist approach to identify the "multiple" realities of the phenomena of serendipitous news discovery perceived by individuals using the active interview (Holstein and Gubrium, 1995) technique to construct the meaning of this ambiguous behavior. Based on in-depth narrative interviews of 20 individuals, this research offers a rich picture of the serendipitous news discovery experience, from the roots of exposure to what is done with the actual content and news, examining behavioral, cognitive, and affective elements involved in the process. Rather than working within the constraints of a single restrictive definition, the constructivist framework allows us to explore a range of views as presented by the study participants about their experiences of serendipity in online news reading. This methodological approach is supported by Makri and Blandford (2012b), who emphasized the importance of recognizing the complexity of serendipity because it is "an inherently subjective phenomenon" that could mean "different things to different people, in different situations" (p. 707). The outcome of the aforementioned process of constructive discovery is the concept of IEON.

## 1.2   STRUCTURE OF THE BOOK

The goals of this book are to investigate the process of IEON, to identify its characteristics as perceived by online news consumers, and to build a rich picture of IEON. The first questions that guide our research include: What is serendipitous news discovery for news consumers? What are their perceptions of this behavior? How does the phenomenon of serendipitous news discovery manifest itself? Where does it take place in everyday life information seeking and news consumption?

If we recognize the existence of serendipity in online news consumption, we must also investigate the process of how it presents itself. The second set of questions we address is: How does the process of IEON happen in an online environment? What are the steps involved in this process? What design elements and content trigger IEON? What kinds of news stories can/do individuals come across online? What is the connection between the encountered news stories and the individual's information needs? Answers to these questions provide a foundation for the IEON process model we propose.

In addition, this book aims to answer the overarching questions about the implications of IEON. Thus, the third part of this book will discuss: How does IEON integrate into individuals' overall news consumption? What are the potential outcomes of IEON? How should the behavior of serendipitous news discovery be defined, studied, measured, and observed? What essential elements differentiate serendipitous news discovery from other news-consuming behaviors online? Could IEON guarantee the expected outcomes for maintaining or even broadening the public sphere as envisioned by communication scholars?

The final part of the book raises important questions about the implications of serendipitous news discovery on a practical level in mass communication: How should the news media position itself and respond to a newly characterized behavior of IEON? In which daily online activities could news potentially be embedded to allow for meaningful serendipitous discovery?

CHAPTER 2

# Literature Review

## 2.1 TRENDS IN NEWS CONSUMPTION

Historically, news consumption has required defined moments in scheduled times and places. As Peters (2015) explained, the practices of journalism were distributed around spatio-temporal routines of newspaper delivery to households before the morning and evening commutes on public transit. Television news was scheduled to suit the transitions of individuals from work to home (early evening news) and home to bed (nightly news) in the living rooms of most houses. With this type of stability and predictability to news consumption, media institutions had much more power to control what news was delivered to their audiences and with greater guarantee of reaching the masses. Therefore, in the early years of media effects research, audience members were considered passive and the media was considered to have a powerful effect on them.

With the uses and gratifications (U&G), Katz (1959) marked the turning point in communication studies. He suggested asking the question "What do people do with the media?" instead of classical inquiry "What do the media do to people?" in media audience studies. This approach is built on the assumptions that people's values, interests, associations, social roles play huge role in what they see and hear to these interests in media messages. McQuail et al. (1972) suggested the following categories of media audience needs and gratifications: diversion—to escape from routine and problems; personal relationships—for social utility of information in conversations and substituting the media for companionship; personal identity—for value reinforcement, self-understanding, and so forth; surveillance—for information about things that might affect one or will help one do or accomplish something. Katz et al. (1973) listed 35 needs taken from the literature on the social and psychological functions of the mass media and divide them into five categories: cognitive, affective, personal integrative, social integrative, and escape-tension-release needs.

In the 1980s, researchers started challenging the basic notions of the U&G approach and argued that exposure to mass media is not always highly deliberate or purposeful. One example is the escapist model of media use, which presumes that people use media, especially TV, to pass time (Barwise et al., 1982). Horna (1988) found that mass media plays a crucial role in fulfilling people's needs for relaxation, recuperation, entertainment, and sociability despite their feelings of guilt over unproductive usage of time.

Rubin (1984) proposed that how audiences use media could be either instrumental or ritualistic. Instrumental use refers to an active, selective, and purposive consumption of certain media content for specific needs, while ritualized use is the habitual consumption of a medium for diffuse motives, such as passing time or relaxation. Rubin suggested that "audience activity is not an absolute concept, but a variable one" (p. 76). He argued that individuals may use media ritualistically or instrumentally depending on background, time, and situational demands. Windahl (1981) argued that audience activity varies across phases of the communication sequence: people tend to display different types and amounts of activity in various settings and at distinctive times in the communication process. Levy and Windahl (1984) proposed that the typology of audience activity was constructed from two orthogonal dimensions: the qualitative orientation of audience members toward the communication process and the temporal dimension having to do with a particular time or phase of the communication sequence. Donohew et al. (1984) emphasized the importance of investigating the automaticity and low-level of attention in media consumption. Severin and Tankard (2001) also argued that media usage could be ritualistic or habitual when people have a low level of attention to media. Other studies have also indicated that many individuals maintain habitual repertoires of media consumption (Yuan, 2011; LaRose, 2010).

Rapid technological and social changes in the past few decades have had an enormous impact on the media industry and on consumers, even further affecting the way people use media. Today, news is being distributed globally in multiple formats and platforms with no geographical and time limitations. Furthermore, news is increasingly "mobile, instantaneous, and available on demand, participatory, personalized, locational and localized" (Peters, 2015, p. 5). Traditional media outlets do not define the communication space anymore. Technological advancements have brought many new competing actors into the media ecology, such as Yahoo! portals, Facebook, Twitter, and Snapchat, all providing an abundance of news and information. Citizens are not passive news recipients any more. They can almost effortlessly produce content themselves and share news on social media. They can also interact with journalists, writers, bloggers, media producers, politicians, companies, musicians, celebrities, friends, and family members in a digital communication space. This massive upheaval of changes in online news consumption raises concerns about the impact of the Internet on maintaining an active citizenry in a democratic society. Groundbreaking changes on both sides of the news distribution system (media outlets and consumers) challenge the historical role of the media in keeping citizens informed about a common core of news and current affairs (Sunstein, 2001; Lee, 2007).

The Internet is offering individuals tremendous control and flexibility in selecting news, based on content that matches their individual interests and needs (Sunstein, 2001), from different geographical locations at their convenience. News consumers have better opportunities for not only greater content diversification but also for increased control over information selection (Kim, 2012; Zillmann et al., 2004). On the other hand, such freedom and flexibility with news selection increases the opportunity for individuals to select mainly entertainment content and avoid serious news. Putnam (1995, 2000) offered cautions about the dangers of the technological transformation that leads people to follow their individual interests rather than collective ones. Prior (2005) reported that new media forms allow certain people to "tune out of politics" completely, making them "apolitical" and less active citizens (p. 587). Scheufele and Nisbet (2002) found that people who use the Internet for entertainment purposes are less aware of current events. They concluded that the Internet has a minimal role in promoting active and informed citizenship.

## 2.2 SERENDIPITY FROM THE PERSPECTIVE OF MEDIA AUDIENCE STUDIES

Despite these concerns related to selective exposure to online news, many communication scholars express hope that the Internet and social media, with their limitless possibilities of content integration, co-creation, and sharing, have intensified incidental exposure to news, whereby individuals "stumble upon" news while they are doing various online activities with no primary intention to read news (Tewksbury et al., 2001; Salwen et al., 2005; Nguyen, 2008; Purcell et al., 2010; Mitchelstein and Boczkowski, 2010; Mitchell et al., 2013; Kim et al., 2013).

A growing number of mass communication researchers have begun to explore IEON. The Pew Internet study (Purcell et al., 2010) suggests that Americans obtain their news via methods based on foraging and opportunism. According to this study, eight out of ten online news users reported that they experience serendipitous news consumption at least a few times a week, including 59% who said that this consumption happens every day or almost every day. Several other studies support the claim that the Internet enables people to discover news unintentionally while they are involved in different online activities (Mitchelstein and Boczkowski, 2010; Nguyen, 2008). Tewksbury et al. (2001) argued that the prevalence of news on the web provides opportunities for people to encounter news in an incidental way as a by-product of their online activities.

The concept of IEON (also called accidental news exposure) is not entirely new in media audience and communication studies. Down (1957) presented the process of incidental learning based on the concept of information cost. He argued that individuals' accidental exposure to information would allow them to obtain information without seeking it, which means with no cost. This way, people could learn about public affairs through incidental learning. Krugman (1965) discussed "learning without involvement" in the context of TV advertising. Krugman and Hartley (1970) recognized that the mass media could offer passive learning among television viewers. He defined passive learning as "typically effortless, responsive to animated stimuli, amenable to artificial aid to relaxation, and characterized by an absence of resistance to what is learned" (p. 184). The concept of incidental learning has been applied in various studies, including political advertising (Brians and Wattenberg, 1996), political entertainment (Feldman and Young, 2008), and soft news content (Baum, 2002; Baum and Jamison, 2006). Brians and Wattenberg (1996) found that political advertising has an impact on citizens' learning about presidential candidates' issue positions. Feldman and Young (2008) found that exposure to late-night comedy is associated with higher levels of attention to the presidential campaign in traditional television news. Baum (2002) reported that politically inattentive individuals are exposed to information about important political issues as a result of an "incidental by-product of seeking entertainment" in media (p. 91). Zukin and Snyder (1984) found that passive learning is a common way for citizens to acquire knowledge about politics while habitually using media.

The majority of studies on IEON in media audiences are based on the concept of incidental learning. The studies typically define serendipitous news discovery based on one or the combination of two approaches: intention-based (encountering news while doing non-news-related activities) and/or topic-based (novelty of news topic). The intention-based definition of serendipitous news discovery assumes that users come across news online while doing activities with no primary intention to read news. The topic-based definition of serendipitous news discovery is based on the premise that users serendipitously find unusual or interesting news on different topics while reading news on topics that interest them.

Tewksbury et al. (2001) used the following two questions from the national surveys of media and communication technology use by the American public, conducted by the Pew Research Center for the People and the Press, to define incidental exposure to news:

- *When you go online, are you ever exposed to news and information on current events, public issues, or politics when you may have been going online for a purpose other than to get news?* (Pew survey from autumn, 1996 cited in Tewskbury et al., p. 548)

- *When you go online, do you ever encounter or come across news and information on current events, public issues, or politics when you may have been going online for a purpose other than to get news?"* (Pew survey from spring and autumn, 1998 cited in Tewskbury et al., p. 548)

These questions attempted to differentiate online activities based on the *initial* purposes of users, regardless of whether they had *any* intention to read news online or not.

In a study of the news consumption of Americans, Purcell et al. (2010) measure serendipitous news consumption with the following survey items:

- *I like coming across news about topics and issues that I have not thought about very much before.* (p. 20)

- *How often do you come across news when you are online doing other things?* (p. 29)

The first item focuses on the topic of encountered news while the second one is tailored to capture the type of activity.

Salwen et al. (2005) found that serendipity is one of four important attributes of online news, along with convenience of use, quantity and quality of news, and difference of online news from traditional news. Their definition of serendipity seems to be based on that of the Pew Research Center, which identifies serendipitous online news exposure as a consequence of general web search, enticements to click to news stories at Internet service providers' (ISPs) websites, and news encountered while searching for non-news information on search engines. They use two survey items to measure serendipity: the type of news (unusual, interesting) and the context in which serendipitous news exposure happened (news stories that caught readers' attention when logging on or logging off the computer). To capture the different types of activities readers were engaged in when exposed to news, their survey also includes specific questions about finding news while logging on and off the computer and finding news on ISP pages. Kim et al. (2013) attempted to differentiate the variety of online activities during which individuals could experience incidental exposure to news, asking specific questions about the types of websites such as search engines, portal sites, forums or listservs, blogs, and social networking sites.

The findings from the early studies of serendipity and news reading produced initial insights into the potential role of this type of news exposure in shaping people's political views and public engagement. For example, a study by Tewksbury et al. (2001) examined the effects of incidental news exposure online on individuals' current affairs knowledge and found that accidental news exposure may have a positive role in informing citizens. Kim et al. (2013) found that unintentional news exposure on the Internet may play a significant role in facilitating people's political participation. Their findings indicate that this positive impact of incidental news exposure on online political participation was stronger for people who prefer news than for people who use the Internet for entertainment. Tian and Robinson (2009) studied incidental media usage in the health communication context. They found that incidental health information use is positively associated with overall Internet use, active health information seeking on the Internet, and incidental health information use from traditional media.

Although the foregoing research indicates an emergence of interest in serendipity in news consumption, there is insufficient systematic understanding about how people conceptualize and experience this new type of news reading. The prominent theories in media research described above do not specifically refer to the existence of unexpected exposure to news. The need for conceptual frameworks to guide a systematic study of serendipity in a news reading context led us to research in the related field of LIS where this phenomenon has been studied within the broader context of human information behavior.

## 2.3   SERENDIPITY RESEARCH IN THE HUMAN INFORMATION BEHAVIOR FIELD

The theoretical and methodological frameworks from serendipitous information retrieval research in the field of information science provide strong foundations to investigate the phenomenon of serendipitous news discovery. Information science scholars started studying human information seeking behavior with studies of readership and library users in the 1920s. Since then, information behavior research has expanded tremendously to encompass different contexts, user groups, and motives. Case (2002) has explained that information behavior, including both active and passive information seeking and information use across channels, is difficult to study because it varies so much across people, situations, and objects of interest and "takes place primarily inside a person's head" (p. 5).

Information science scholars stress the importance of studying human information behavior from a holistic perspective, examining behavioral, cognitive, and affective dimensions, although the many observable and unobservable behaviors related to how people seek and use information make this challenging. Savolainen (2007) noted the challenge of combining internal and external components of information behavior and specifying how unobservable cognitive behavior affects and orients observable information behavior and vice versa. Nahl (2005) suggested that researchers need to look at both the affective and cognitive mental activity of information users, since "thinking of a search word" or "feeling motivated to finish a task" are parts of their behavior (p. 39).

Research on serendipity in information seeking includes examining this phenomenon from the perspective of different user populations and various domains of information activities. The terms used to identify these types of behavior are as follows: IE (Erdelez, 1997), opportunistic acquisition of information (Erdelez, 2005), opportunistic discovery of information (Erdelez and Makri, 2011), incidental acquisition of information (Williamson, 1998; Heinström, 2006), or simply serendipity (Sun et al., 2011). Serendipity in information seeking has been studied across older adults (Williamson, 1998), architects (Makri and Warwick, 2010), reading for pleasure (Ross, 1999), reading electronic news (Toms, 2000), and everyday life (Rubin et al., 2011). Information science researchers have examined psychological factors of incidental information acquisition (Heinström, 2006), the effect of personalized search results on the potential for serendipitous encounters (André et al., 2009), and the connection between purposive information seeking and serendipitous information discovery (Pálsdóttir, 2009).

Similar to their mass media and communication colleagues, LIS researchers have not so far reached consensus on the conceptual definition of this behavior. Serendipity is described as "random, elusive, and unpredictable" (McBirnie, 2008), "slippery" (Makri and Blandford, 2012a), and "hard to capture and induce" (Erdelez, 2004). However, one pattern that has emerged is that research on serendipity in information behavior seems to emphasize not merely the accidental and unexpected nature of this behavior but also the expectation of positive or fortuitous outcomes (Cunha et al., 2010; Rubin et al., 2011; Makri and Blandford, 2012b). For example, Makri and Blandford (2012b) found that researchers' own serendipitous experiences involved a mix of unexpectedness and insight that led to valuable, unanticipated outcomes.

## 2.4 INFORMATION ENCOUNTERING

Erdelez (1997) recognized the existence of the unexpected and accidental discovery of useful or interesting information when users look for specific information (i.e., looking for books in the library catalog) or during browsing activity when one "gathers information while scanning an information space without an explicit purpose" (p. 423). She identified four dimensions to investigate this behavior: *information user* (who encountered information), *environment* (setting in which information was encountered), *information* (what was encountered), and *information need* (the need addressed with encountered information).

The *user dimension* encompasses behavioral, cognitive, and affective elements of the information encounter as experienced by information users. To examine these elements, she asked users what activities they were doing prior to and after IE. She categorized the activities performed immediately before IE as either *information-related* or *non-information-related*. Cognitive and affective aspects of the user dimension were examined by comparing thoughts and feelings experienced by respondents immediately before and immediately after the IE. Under user dimension, Erdelez (1997) identified four different types of information encounterers:

- *Super-encounterers*: those who rely on bumping into information as a method for information acquisition and often encounter information related to them;

- *Encounterers*: those who often come across information but do not see a connection between information encountering and other aspects of their information behavior;

- *Occasional Encounterers*: those who sometimes encounter information but do not see this as more than luck; and

- *Non-Encounterers*: those who seldom experience encountering information (p. 417).

The personal characteristics of super-encounterers included "curiosity, desire for exploration, [and] interest in different hobbies and various subject areas" (Erdelez, 1997, p. 417).

The *information environment* dimension encompasses physical places and information sources where users encounter information. Erdelez and Rioux (2000) stated that IE can be experienced in various environments, including "libraries and retail environments, on the web, while watching TV, or during any other type of human activity that broadly involves information behavior" (p. 220).

Having analyzed the nature of the information encountered, Erdelez divided the encountered content into problem-related and interest-related. Problem-related information was useful and applicable to some identifiable areas, such as finding a hotel room. Interest-related information addressed some areas of "general interest or concern," and its usefulness was vague (Erdelez, 1997, p. 416).

Erdelez classified *information needs* associated with IE into three groups: present, future, and past needs of individuals. She found that the majority of needs related to IE addressed present needs on respondents' list of things to do. Only a few IE experiences addressed future information needs, such as the need to attend a certain event in the future. Erdelez (1997) also found that individuals not only address their own information needs but also the needs of others.

Erdelez (2000) studied information encountering on the web and concluded that the "serendipitous or accidental discovery of information is not some second-rate, haphazard behavior but a form of information acquisition complementary to other active and problem-specific types of information behavior" (p. 369). In a follow-up study, Erdelez and Rioux (2000) identified that even short Internet sessions might trigger IE experiences that result in useful information for users themselves and others, given the richness of this environment. They found that users are "excited when they accidentally come across information useful to others while they are on the web and they feel good about helping others by sharing this information" (p. 227). The most common sharing method was copying and pasting URL links in email messages and adding a personal note. Their findings highlighted the fact that information encountering could address not only the needs of the user who encounters a given piece of information, but also the needs of other people (e.g., friends, family, co-workers). Erdelez's (2000) initial model of Information Encountering identified the "functional components" of an information encountering episode:

- Noticing: unexpected information catches user's attention;

- Stopping: temporarily diverted from some other activity that was under way, user attends to the information encountered;

- Examination: user becomes involved in the information encountered, by reading it or exploring it in some other way;

- Storing: user mentally or physically saves the information for some future use;

- Use: encountered information is used for personal needs and/or shared with others;

- Returning: user returns to the activity that was interrupted with IE (p. 369).

Erdelez's (2004) revised IE model (Figure 2.1) focused on active information seeking. This new model assumes that information users switch from the foreground task of finding specific information to a background interest or problem-related task during the IE process. Accordingly, Erdelez slightly changed the description of the steps involved in IE:

- Noticing: the perception of encountered information;

- Stopping: the interruption of the initial information seeking activity;

- Examining: the assessment of usefulness of the encountered information;

- Capturing: the extraction and saving of the encountered information for future use;

- Returning: the reconnection with the initial information seeking task (p. 1015).

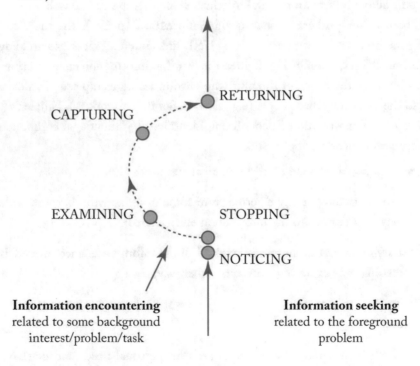

Figure 2.1: IE Model (Erdelez, 2004).

The steps described as Storing and Use in her previous model (Erdelez, 2000) were changed to the Capturing step. Erdelez noted that the described steps may not necessarily be present in each IE episode, because "the mode of their fulfillment will depend on the characteristics of the specific information environment" (p. 1015). She also recognized the possibility that IE occurrences could be facilitated by the "parallel presence of various situations in people's everyday lives that can be defined very broadly as problems," each with different levels of specificity, urgency, and complexity (p. 1015). People's information needs depend on these discrete problems, which causes them to switch to the background problems in their minds even during active searches for information not related to those problems. Given the limitations of the human perceptual system when seeking information, a person typically attends to only one problem at a time (Erdelez, 2004).

This study explores IEON from a holistic perspective including social, behavioral, cognitive, and affective dimensions, based on the dissertation data collected by the first author. We applied Erdelez's (1997) conceptual framework of IE, which provides theoretical and methodological guidance to investigate the ambiguous nature of serendipitous news discovery. This study also aims to evaluate the IE model (Erdelez, 2000) in the process of serendipitous news discovery because this model encompasses both active information seeking and browsing, which are applicable in online news reading behavior. The present study proposes that online news consumption happens in an ELIS context (Savolainen, 1995) and that people read online news both actively with a certain goal and passively without predetermined goals.

# CHAPTER 3

# Methods

## 3.1    STUDY DESIGN METHODS

In order to capture respondents' subjective explanations of their IEON behavior, we employed an explanatory mixed method design (Creswell and Clark, 2007), which uses qualitative data to build upon initial quantitative results. This design is suitable when the researcher uses quantitative participant characteristics to guide purposeful sampling for a qualitative phase.

We first used surveys to collect data on respondents' general news reading behavior and their self-awareness regarding IEON. Quantitative data provided a general picture of news consumers' online news reading behavior. To find people who read news online, we applied purposeful and convenience sampling (Lincoln and Guba, 1985) for this study. The logic and power of purposeful sampling is derived from the emphasis on in-depth understanding, leading to information-rich cases (Patton, 2002). We recruited participants through the website of the local Columbia, Missouri, newspaper the *Columbia Missourian* by and through email invitations via the mailing lists of several local institutions. Through this process, we collected 146 completed and valid questionnaires. Two-thirds of the survey respondents (67%) were over the age of 31; about 23% were over the age of 51; and only 2% were under the age of 20. By gender, the pool of respondents was more female (60%) than male (40%). Just over half of the respondents (52%) reported that they had graduate or professional degrees, followed by 19% with four-year college degrees and 18% with some college-level education. The Internet was their dominant source for news gathering. About 73% of respondents reported that they "always" use the Internet as a primary source of news events and 27% said they do this "sometimes." Friends were reported as the second-most prominent source of news, followed by radio. About 59% of respondents to this question said they "sometimes" get informed about news events from their friends, and about 34% reported they "always" use radio to get informed about news. Due to the sampling method employed in this study, our findings are not generalizable beyond the study sample.

Descriptive statistical analysis of the survey helped us select a diverse group of individuals to follow up with in the qualitative part of this study. We selected the interview respondents based on their level of awareness about their IEON experiences. Four questions in the survey were designed to measure the self-awareness of respondents regarding their IEON in two different contexts: (1) while browsing news online, or (2) during other non-news related activities. Based on the survey feedback we attempted to identify the four types of information encounterers as categorized by Erdelez (1997): super-encounterers, encounterers, occasional encounterers, and non-encounterers. The majority of survey respondents reported that they experience serendipitous news discovery "very often" or "often." Three-quarters of the respondents said they "very often" or "fairly often" come across interesting news stories online when they browse the Internet for other purposes than news reading. Seventy-eight percent reported that they find interesting news stories at times when they browse the news websites without a specific goal in mind. Because the majority of responses were on the higher end of the scale (options "very often" or "often"), we decided to conduct follow-up interviews with respondents equally represented from both categories of responses. In order to get rich and diverse feedback from respondents, the additional criteria for the selection of interview participants were the news reading and non-news reading context of IEON, the top five online news sources they used, and demographic variables (e.g., age, gender, ethnicity, education).

The in-depth interviews were conducted with 20 respondents with the application of a critical incident technique (Flanagan, 1954), explication interviews (Urquhart et al., 2003), and think-aloud (Nielsen, 1993) methods. All interviews were recorded with Morae 3.0, a software that can capture audio and video input, and also interactions with the computer. To suit the needs of the respondents, two of the interview sessions were conducted at the home and the office of the respective respondents. The remaining 18 interviews took place in a university information experience laboratory.

Consistent with core principles of grounded theory, we continued to interview respondents and analyze data until we reached saturation (Glaser and Strauss, 1967). Selection of interview respondents aimed to include the maximum variation of information-rich cases and to reach a point of theoretical saturation, which refers to the (non)emergence of new properties, categories, or relationships. Once the body of data no longer offered new distinctions of conceptual import, categories were described as "saturated," and no further evidence about experiences of IEON in daily news consumption was collected (Dey, 1999). The main goal of this study was not to find generalizable results but to get a deeper understanding about news consumers' IEON experiences.

About 40% of the interview respondents were male and 60% of them were female. The majority of the interview respondents (70%) were between the ages of 20 and 40; about 25% were over the age of 40; and only 5% of them were under the age of 20. The majority of the interview respondents (70%) stated that they have some graduate work and/or a graduate/professional degree. About 40% were students, 5% were employed part time, and 55% were employed full time. Appendix 1 provides basic demographics of the interview respondents. For confidentiality reasons, each respondent was coded with an "R" followed by an assigned number.

Each interview session started with the critical incident technique and then proceeded with an explication interview and think-aloud method. We identified the critical incident technique developed by Flanagan during his work in the U.S. Army Air Forces Aviation Psychology Program (1954) as a flexible set of principles that could be modified for the investigation of IEON. This technique is used "to collect data on observations previously made which are reported from memory (Flanagan, 1954, p. 339). The main goal of this method is to obtain recent incidents to insure that they are representative of actual happenings of certain behavior. We also used the explication interviewing technique developed by Vermersch (1994), drawing on Piaget's theory of how experience is processed into reflection. The technique seeks to help people progress from a pre-reflected to a reflected experience and is thus relevant for studying IEON. We determined that the think-aloud method (Nielsen, 1993), commonly used for psychological research and in evaluation of human-computer interfaces, could further enrich our data. The key point of this method is to engage the participants with the actual information activity and to ask them to verbally reflect their thoughts, feelings, and actions.

During the critical incident portion of the interview, we asked respondents to take a moment and attempt to recall their most recent experience of stumbling upon a news story online. Further, we asked them to elicit the details of each incident: how this incident happened, what story they came across, and what activities they were doing when they stumbled upon the news story. Some of these questions were adapted from interview guides Erdelez (1995) used in her study of IE.

When respondents began sharing their critical incident stories of IEON, they were asked to share information about their general tendency to stumble on information and to define IEON in their daily news reading context. Because respondents had various perceptions of IEON, we attempted to reach a common ground in terms of understanding IEON with the use of active interview technique (Holstein and Gubrium, 1995). Respondents were asked how, where, and how often they experienced IEON and how they felt about this experience. Once they gained an understanding of

IEON, they were able to elaborate more about their general tendency to be exposed to news incidentally and the places and frequency of this behavior.

During think-aloud sessions, the respondents were situated in front of desktop computers. We asked them to engage in online news reading and take us through their typical routine. This process attempted to capture in real time potential IEON experiences and also facilitate recall of specific IEON episodes reported in respondents' critical incident stories. The respondents we also encouraged to identify specific interface design features that triggered IEON. The Morae software enabled us to capture respondents' immediate interactions with the online news sites, providing a recording of their reactions and many nuances about their IEON, online news reading behavior, and trigger elements for IEON in general.

## 3.2   DATA ANALYSIS

Qualitative data from the 20 interviews were fully transcribed electronically through a professional transcription service. All transcripts were imported to QSR NVivo 8.0, a qualitative data analysis software package. We analyzed the three parts of the qualitative data (critical incident stories, general interviews, think-aloud sessions) separately and performed data triangulation. The direct quotes that appear in this book were edited for clarity of expression and readability.

The main goal of the qualitative data analysis was to find the emergent themes relevant to the research questions aimed at exploring the nature of IEON in the ELIS context. The key concepts from the IE conceptual framework were used in a deductive analysis process. The grounded theory approach (Strauss and Corbin, 1998) was used to analyze qualitative data by means of inductive analysis. This approach was chosen as the most appropriate analytic strategy for the present study because it allows the development of the coding scheme to be informed both by existing theoretical models and by the data itself. We employed open coding, axial coding, and constant comparison techniques (Corbin and Strauss, 2008), using existing and emerging codes. Corbin and Strauss (2008) have described "constant comparison" as the process of comparing each incident in the data with other "incidents for similarities and differences" (p. 73).

CHAPTER 4

# Perception of IEON

The first set of questions that guided our research includes: How does the phenomenon of serendipitous news discovery manifest itself, and where does it take place in everyday news consumption? What is serendipitous news discovery for news consumers? What are their perceptions of this behavior?

## 4.1 ONLINE NEWS CONSUMERS AND THEIR PERCEPTION OF IEON

The evidence from 25 critical incident cases of IEON experiences (Table 4.1) and interviews with think-aloud sessions revealed that individuals' perceptions of IEON are based on both their perceptions of news and their online news consumption habits.

| ID | Example of the IEON Incident |
|----|------------------------------|
| | Table 4.1: Summary of IEON incidents |
| R1 | Encountered a news story about the local lady who helps newcomers to the city at local newspaper's website. |
| R2 | Incident 1: Encountered a YouTube award situation in Saint Louis at local newspaper's site.<br>Incident 2: Encountered a story about alleged gun fighting in local city park while she was reading local newspaper's website. |
| R3 | Encountered a story about gay marriage in Iowa at *The New York Times* website while he was sitting in economics class. |
| R4 | Encountered a story about the trial of the Pirate Bay (a site for illegal downloading of TV shows and movies in Europe) at Boing Boing site during his ritualistic news reading in the morning. |
| R5 | Encountered a story about the merger of Sun Microsystems with Oracle in his email during his habitual email checking in the morning. Clicked on a story and went to Ning social networking site. |
| R6 | Encountered a story about an 11-year-old boy who was bullied and committed suicide at CNN.com site while he was multitasking on his computer. |
| R7 | Encountered a story about the rescue of a captain by Navy Seals when she went to local newspaper's site to check classifieds on furniture. |

| | |
|---|---|
| R8 | Encountered a story about the changes in teachers' jobs in the local school in Indianapolis, where he lived before moving to the city. He had a goal to sell his house and visited the *Indianapolis Star* newspaper's site. |
| R9 | Incident 1: Encountered a story about the entertainer who was mentioned in the conversation with her spouse when she went online later in the evening.<br>Incident 2: Encountered news/information about project management in her email while doing work-related email communication.<br>Incident 3: Heard news about a swine flu outbreak on the radio while driving.<br>Incident 4: Heard about the pandemic's spread of swine flu from colleague first and checked online at *The New York Times* when she got on her computer. |
| R10 | Encountered a story about the newly elected president of South Africa being a polygamist at morningnews.com while he was taking a break during his work. |
| R11 | Incident 1: Encountered a story about the top five things about H1N1 not to panic over while she was checking her own portal with RSS feeds from news organizations.<br>Incident 2: Heard about a story about immigrants on radio, then she followed up this story online. |
| R12 | Encountered a story about President Barack Obama's judicial nomination of Judge David Hamilton to the United States 7th Circuit Court of Appeals in subscribed email from NewsMatch.com during her evening routine on the Internet. |
| R13 | Encountered a headline about an interview with Douglas Rushkoff, an advocate of local currencies, on Google Reader during his break on computer. |
| R14 | Encountered a story about the probation of the university health center while she was checking local newspaper's website looking for a story about a shooting on campus. |
| R15 | Encountered a story about the first anniversary of an earthquake in China while browsing the news on Next China, a news site for Chinese people living abroad. |
| R16 | Encountered a story about Sarah Palin's (vice presidential candidate in 2008 U.S. elections) reputation at Digg.com during her morning routine of checking news sites as a break from work. |

| R17 | Encountered a news story about Susan Boyle (a Scottish singer who came to international public attention when she appeared as a contestant on the British reality TV program *Britain's Got Talent*) at the Yahoo! homepage when she went to this site to check her email. |
|-----|---|
| R18 | Encountered a story about the student with swine flu while she was checking her email. |
| R19 | Encountered a story about how the Chinese government is handling a swine flu case at the *Christian Science Monitor* website while he was writing a research paper on his computer. |
| R20 | Encountered a story about the divorce controversy from the TV reality-show *John and Kate Plus 8* when she checked her Hotmail account at the MSN site. |

## 4.1.1 THE TYPES OF NEWS STORIES INDIVIDUALS COME ACROSS ONLINE

We analyzed the encountered news stories in terms of their content, source, and geographical emphasis. The following eight themes were identified as topics of incidentally exposed news stories:

1. personal safety (5 cases)

2. politics (5)

3. entertainment/leisure (4)

4. technology (3)

5. business (3)

6. crime (1)

7. education (1)

8. disaster (1)

The five cases related to personal safety involved stories about swine flu, which was a prominent issue during the time frame of study data collection. Stories about swine flu were mostly related to spread of this disease. Five respondents reported that they were incidentally exposed to political news stories, including gay marriage regulation, loss of popularity of a political candidate, U.S. Supreme Court nomination, hostage rescue, and a backlash against Mexican immigrants.

## 4.1.2  THE TYPES OF ONLINE NEWS SOURCES AS AN ENVIRONMENT FOR IEON

Respondents shared that they came across news through the following types of sources: websites of traditional news media organizations, email, news sites not affiliated with mainstream media (alternative media sources on the Internet), social networking sites, and sources outside of the Internet.

The news stories reported in critical incident stories originated from a variety of sources:

- Local newspaper websites: *Columbia Daily Tribune*, *Indianapolis Star*;

- National newspaper websites: *The New York Times*, *Christian Science Monitor*;

- Websites for specific communities (professional and ethnic): Ning, Chinese community website;

- National TV websites: CNN, MSNBC;

- News portals: MSN, Yahoo!;

- Alternative online news sources: Digg, Boing Boing, News Match, The Morning News (http://www.themorningnews.org);

- Radio;

- Other: spouse, friend, Google reader, email.

Of the events described in the news stories, 2 stories were local, 12 were national, and 9 were international. One local news story concerned a local woman who helped connect the business community of Columbia, Missouri, to newcomers to the area. The other local story featured a teacher making changes in a community (Indianapolis, Indiana) where the respondent (R8) previously lived.

## 4.1.3  THE TYPES OF ONLINE NEWS READERS

Responses suggested that while some respondents still identify news as tied to traditional media, others hold a much broader perception of news that goes beyond what is reported by professional journalists. This latter category of respondents considered every piece of information they found online as news, and some considered anything that enhances their understanding of events happening in the world as news. A few respondents perceived news in terms of information related to their work and professional needs.

A detailed analysis of respondents' online news consumption revealed four types of news readers: *avid news readers, news avoiders, news encounterers,* and *crowd surfers.* These types were based on respondents' news consumption habits, irrespective of education, occupation, and other demographic variables.

*Avid news readers* follow their lifelong habits in reading news. They have established habits of checking a number of online news sites affiliated with professional news organizations, including the websites of local, hometown, and national newspapers and radio and TV channels. Some of them also follow Facebook and Twitter feeds of these news organizations and receive RSS feeds in their email. Avid news readers trust traditional media more than the other three types of news readers.

*News avoiders* do not follow the general news events covered by the mainstream media or visit alternative news sources or aggregate news websites. They try to avoid major news outlets because the negative news that dominates in these channels makes them upset, depressed, frustrated, and angry. They feel a lack of control over the events covered in the news and would rather spend their time focusing on job- and hobby- or interest-related information. In many cases these people reported getting news from their spouses and friends, who served as filters of undesirable news.

*News encounterers* have no established habit of checking certain news sources on a daily basis. Unlike avid news readers, their online news reading is random and depends much on the stories they encounter in different contexts, both online and in their physical environments with radio and personal communication. This group of news consumers truly enjoys the richness of Internet content. They take advantage of any opportunity to gain exposure to news on the Internet.

*Crowd surfers* read news on sites such as Digg because they believe in the *wisdom of the crowd.* They read "newsworthy" stories voted on by visitors to the site rather than relying on the stories selected by journalists. They are very critical of mainstream media news coverage and check for spin in news stories, reading comments and discussion related to news stories.

### 4.1.4  PERCEPTION OF IEON

Respondents used the following expressions to describe their IEON experience: encounter/come across/stumble upon news, accidental discovery of news, serendipitous discovery of a news story, find news unintentionally/accidentally, bump into some news unexpectedly, finding out unexpected knowledge/result, finding random things that one would not expect.

Many respondents explained that IEON happens as something interesting "catches their eye." Most stated that they were not aware of this behavior prior to our interviews. Once their attention was drawn to IEON, they commented that this is a very common experience, but they typically do not actively think about the process of how it happens.

At the other end of the spectrum of awareness level, there were a few respondents who said they intentionally experienced IEON from sites such as the *Drudge Report*, Gawker, Yahoo! portals, Digg, Boing Boing, Slate, and StumbleUpon. These nontraditional news sites have "inflammatory" and "obvious" headlines (R11), with "a ton of random links," which allowed respondents to find "interesting things" just by "clicking on something" (R14).

Most respondents tried to define IEON based on their presence or lack of intention to find news while coming across it serendipitously. However, the concept of *intention* itself received different interpretations. A few respondents felt strongly that the meaning of IEON should be restricted to experiences when the intention of the primary activity was not related to news reading. These respondents defined IEON as coming across news when they were doing "something not related to news," such as checking email or visiting social media sites. R17, for example, defined IEON as "seeing news" while she is doing something else, mainly on the Yahoo! site. R5 similarly said that he would not consider anything found while browsing Digg (http://digg.com) as IEON because he is "actually expecting to run into unexpected information," compared to expecting a "business as usual experience" while checking his email, where he does not come across unexpected information. Conversely, other respondents perceived IEON in the news browsing context and included experiences of coming across unexpected, unusual, or interesting news items while they visited online news sites. R1 said that she came across a news story about the local lady who helps newcomers to the city when she was browsing the website of the local newspaper. R2 also reported encountering a story about alleged gun fighting in a local city park during her ritualistic visit to the local newspaper's website. Finally, a couple of respondents pointed out that everything they do on the Internet leads to IEON because of the nature of the Internet. This explanation is related to the information architecture of the Internet, which provides a very information-rich environment and blurs the boundaries of media sources.

The above two types of perceptions of IEON could be attributed to differing perceptions of news itself, which in turn affects news consumption behaviors and the sources of news people use in their daily lives. The four types of news consumers (avid news readers, news avoiders, news encounterers, and crowd surfers) show how the potential outcomes of IEON could vary in diversity, quality, and volume of news consumed. As compared to avid news readers, who mainly consume news from a limited number of often traditional media news sites, the other three groups of news consumers have better opportunities to be exposed to news from different sources.

Respondents' perceptions of IEON could be thus divided into two groups: (1) IEON in a news reading context—finding unexpected, unusual, off-the-wall, bizarre news during news browsing, and (2) IEON in a non-news-reading context—finding news during non-news-related online activities (email checking, visiting social networking sites).

## 4.2    IEON IN A NEWS READING CONTEXT

Respondents perceived IEON in a news reading context when they found unusual, curiosity-piquing, or knowledge-enhancing information during their regular online news browsing process. These people typically belong to a category of avid news readers or crowd surfers. While some respondents followed their habit of reading news online at certain times of the day, others went to the news sites while looking for a mental break or for an escape from boredom. Compared to news avoiders, these respondents were not as sensitive to news events and reported real joy in IEON experiences, likening it to "discovering treasure."

Many respondents reported that IEON simply happens when something catches their eye, but only some were consciously aware of this behavior. R9 said that while she experiences IEON pretty frequently, she does not think about its process. The absence of meta-cognitive awareness made it difficult for respondents to define IEON, as illustrated by R2, who said "sometimes, something happens and I didn't know it happened," and that sometimes stories are "just so outrageous that you just have to look."

Surprise and strong emotional responses emerged as major factors differentiating IEON from typical news browsing. Respondents in this group defined IEON as finding *unusual, weird, interesting, bizarre, unexpected, eye-catching, outrageous,* or *off-the-wall* news. For example, R4 constantly stumbles upon news stories at Boing Boing and Slashdot. He commented that Slashdot focuses on technology and science, but it also has content that "just gets thrown in about random things you really wouldn't expect," while Boing Boing focuses on absurdity and oddity. R4 explained that he never knows what is going to be on these sites and often finds "weird" news. Likewise, R3 said he mainly reads national newspapers online, but he also visits the gossip news site Gawker, which he described as his "guilty pleasure." He explained that he reads this site to be informed about news that "everyone was talking about" and added that by reading only *The New York Times* and the *Washington Post*, he would not be exposed to these type of news stories.

Many cases of IEON occurred when respondents followed news stories on topics they were curious about. These respondents conceptualized IEON as encountering news stories about topics that they *did not know*, *did not hear about before*, or *had missed reading*. For example, R4 reported that, while on Boing Boing, he encountered a news story about a site for illegal downloading of TV shows and movies. He commented that he was expecting to find such news at some point, but he did not actively "seek out" this particular story knowing that it would find him eventually. R16 shared that, during a break from work, she browsed through news headlines and came across a link to a news story about vice presidential candidate Sarah Palin at Digg.com that took her to *The Huffington Post*. She was able to have this IEON experience because she was not looking for anything specific. If she was actively "searching for something" she may not have clicked on the unrelated story link. Similarly, R6 said that he stumbles upon news when he visits the websites of MSNBC and CNN, although he very rarely goes there for "a specific purpose."

Only in a few cases did the respondents come across an unexpected news story while visiting online news sites to look for specific information or news stories. R14 heard from her husband about a gunman on the campus and was concerned about her safety. While looking for the news story about the gunman, she found on the same website a list of other stories and then clicked on a link to a different, unrelated story about the health center.

## 4.3   IEON IN A NON-NEWS-READING CONTEXT

Perception of IEON in a *non-news-reading context* means that people unintentionally find news while engaged in activity unrelated to news reading, such as checking email messages, visiting social networking sites, and so on. This pattern was most visible among news encounterers who stated that their online news reading is random and happens mostly through IEON. They stated that given the abundance of information on the Internet, seeking out news intentionally is no long necessary. They have a feeling of being inundated with media and "constantly being shot with news." News encounterers acknowledged that news is so widespread on the Internet that almost everything is incidental because they run into "a thousand headlines" daily.

For example, R14 stated that she does not seek news but mostly relies on IEON. She said she gets news from Yahoo! or MSNBC portals and sometimes clicks on interesting links in Facebook when there is a status update about some news topic. She does not usually go directly to news websites unless her husband sends her direct links.

R9 shared that she does not need to look for news because she lives in a very dynamic and media-rich environment that allows her to stumble across information. She called this media environment "too extreme" and news "so fragmented." The constant presence of overwhelming news gives her the feeling of living in an "attention deficit disorder society" with too many opportunities for stumbling upon things and makes it difficult to focus. R9 expects IEON to be the typical way she gets her daily news. She defined IEON as "a kind of serendipitous discovery of news stories," which is propelled by advertisers, who are trying to say "hey, look over here, this is more interesting." She explained that through IEON she discovers news that she was not aware of otherwise.

R17, a 25-year-old graduate student, also described IEON as her standard way to get the news. She said that she doesn't need to search for news, because every time she checks her email, she glances at Yahoo! news and finds the top news of the day. She also comes across news stories on Facebook when her friends post links to news stories or in the office from contacts with her co-workers.

R18, a 38-year-old professor of medicine, also does not read online news actively by going directly to specific news websites. Instead, she stays informed about daily news by listening to the radio when she drives and also comes across news on the Internet. She reported that she is "oblivious" to news unless she is incidentally exposed to it. Once some news catches her attention, her behavior changes from passive to active and she follows up the news stories on CNN and in *The New York Times*. Time-saving seemed to be a major factor in her news reading behavior because she feels that getting news through IEON wastes less time.

IEON is also the main way to get news for news avoiders. R14 said she does not search for news. because mainstream media covers too many depressing stories. R13, a 25-year-old web developer, tries to stay away from the news from the major news networks and instead finds it on blogs and social networking tools, which provide links to ongoing events from people in a specific location. He gets exposed to news "incidentally" through Twitter feeds by different people and stories posted in places like Boing Boing. He appreciates this type of news exposure directly from other people's perspectives rather than from "fair and balanced" media "hidden behind [a] mask," such as CNN, which has "their filter of perception."

Compared to respondents who experienced IEON in a news reading context, respondents who encountered news while completing unrelated activities clearly defined IEON based on the initial intention of news reading. R18 noted that she would not consider finding interesting news on an online news site to be IEON, because she goes there "with the intent to find out" what she didn't know. She added that IEON is information that she did not look for, something which "catches" her eye. She recalled incidentally seeing a news story about how a fellow student was infected by swine flu while visiting home in China. She found this story on a website following a link from her email while she was looking up information for her education.

## 4.4    EMOTIONAL DIMENSION OF IEON

We asked the respondents about their thoughts and feelings toward IEON after they shared their critical incident stories. Nineteen out of 20 respondents said that they have positive feelings about this behavior and described their feelings and experiences as "lucky," "exciting," "happy," "wonderful," "fun," and "amusing." They said that they "love" and "enjoy" IEON.

Some respondents noted the impact of the event described in the encountered news because of connections to their personal life, work, family, and community. The story about the 11-year-old boy's suicide was particularly provoking to R6. During news reading, he thought about himself, particularly his own experiences "growing up and maturing." This story also led to thoughts of the experiences of his future children, whom R6 hoped would never be so seriously bullied. R15 was happy to read about construction work after the earthquake in China, but at the same time she was worried about the quality of the buildings in case the area had another bad earthquake.

Due to the nature of encountered news content and its outcomes, the memorability of the experience distinguished IEON behavior from typical and habitual news consumption. Emotions associated with IEON play a prominent role in the outcomes and satisfaction of respondents. The respondents felt excited to find a news item that corresponded to their interests, satisfied when the news item confirmed their values, or reassured when it comforted their worries. They felt socially empowered by finding out more about current topics of debate or empathic when they encountered news stories with which they identified. The surprise element of the unexpected encounter strengthened the emotional reaction to news. They described obtaining potential beneficial outcomes from reading the news stories they came across. These include emotional outcomes (Yadamsuren and Heinström, 2011), gaining knowledge, making personal connections, changing perspectives, and others.

CHAPTER 5

# The Process of IEON

Our next task was to examine the process of IEON by focusing on the behavioral, cognitive, and affective characteristics associated with this behavior with the help of the IE model developed by Erdelez (2000) and introduced in Chapter 1.

## 5.1 TRIGGERS FOR IEON

The most prominent trigger elements leading to IEON were eye-catching and/or captivating headlines. The respondents followed their browsing strategies to scan certain specifically designated areas on news sites, such as "most popular," "most read," "most emailed," "most viewed," related links, and top stories. Respondents also mentioned the following design elements: photos, pictures, fonts, headlines, videos, sponsored links, and links to affiliated websites. The actual physical location of news elements appeared to have considerable impact on chance encounters with news online. Respondents also reported finding the IEON triggers at various locations on the website: right-side, center, top, third column, and bottom links. Respondents stated that certain labels for news sections and stories catch their attention and serve as starting points for their IEON experiences. These special spots included the right side on the CNN website, related links, top stories, "most popular," "most read," "most emailed," and "most viewed" parts of the online news sites. While some respondents use these specific locations to navigate and browse online news sites, others pay attention to these areas for social needs to converse about important news events.

R10 reported that he "scrolls through the most popular, the most read, the most emailed, etc.," and "rolls down to see" if he missed something on previous days on news sites. This process ends when he makes sure that he looked through all of these content areas. R3 described how trigger elements differ on various newspaper sites. For example, at *The New York Times* site, he usually goes through all of "the most popular" parts. Whereas at the *Los Angeles Times*, he ignores different labels to read news.

R6 said he encounters the stories at the right sidebar on the CNN website and at the "related stories" section on the bottom of the website. He said he clicks on those links to see what the Top Ten stories are, even if he is not really interested. In a critical incident story, R6 recalled stumbling upon a sad news story about an 11-year-old boy who committed suicide after being bullied. He said he typically tries to avoid those stories to be in a good mood, but since this story was the number one most read story, it attracted his attention.

Several respondents commented that looking at the "most read" or "most emailed" areas helps in social conversations with their colleagues and friends. According to R3, reading the stories in those sections is "a way to find a story that everyone else thinks is really cool and everyone's emailing to each other and commenting on."

## 5.2   STEPS INVOLVED IN IEON

Our findings indicate that all steps (Noticing, Stopping, Examining, Capturing, and Returning) described in the IE model were observed in the IEON process. In addition, we found two steps (Sharing and Wandering Off) that should be added for an IEON process model. In addition, the Examining step from the IE model was changed to a Reading step because we found that assessment of encountered information happens throughout the IEON process and serves as an important factor in the decision-making process for further steps.

### 5.2.1   NOTICING

IEON experience starts with Noticing certain triggers or cues in the online environment. This is an important step in IEON as it determines whether an individual pursues serendipitous news discovery. On a website, a trigger for IEON is often some element of visual design (e.g., photo, image, font color) or structure (e.g., headlines, labels, links). An additional aspect of a trigger that facilitates the process of noticing is the connection between the content of the news story and the interests of the news readers.

Six major themes emerged in our data about the content that triggers IEON: urgency of the news story, personal relevance, professional needs, values and beliefs, sense of community, and bizarre news. We will illustrate each of these themes with examples from the critical incident reports.

**Urgency of the News Story**

A number of respondents paid attention to certain news stories because of their urgency. Four respondents stated that they were incidentally exposed to stories about the swine flu. However, each respondent seemed to have different needs for reading the given news story about this subject. During her morning news reading, R11 noticed a headline on the CNN site concerning the top five things about H1N1 not to panic over. With a sense of urgency, she followed up on the swine flu story because she wanted to know whether she should buy groceries and other items to last for two weeks.

## Personal Relevance

R7 visited the local newspaper's website to look for furniture and encountered a story about the rescue by Navy Seals of a ship captain held hostage. She said that any news story on a military topic typically catches her attention because her husband served in the military for 12 years and her son was joining soon. Because of that, she felt compelled to keep up with events involving the military. She was already familiar with the Navy Seals story and was pleased that the news story she encountered included some additional detail, which put the narrative "in a different light" in comparison with other news sources.

R8 was looking to sell his house in Indianapolis and during his daily routine of visiting the *Indianapolis Star* for this purpose, he incidentally found a news story about the changes in teachers' jobs. Because he used to live and work as a teacher in the area, he was drawn to the story out of concern for the job security of his former colleagues.

## Professional Needs

In many cases, IEON was triggered when respondents noticed some news stories that resonated with their professional interest. R5, a 32-year-old technology project coordinator, reported that he happened to come across a news story about the merger of Oracle and Sun Microsystems while following a link provided in an email to the Ning social networking site. This story was critical for his work because he used tools developed by Sun and worried whether Oracle was going to continue to invest resources into development of the software he used.

R4 encountered a news story on Boing Boing about the verdict in a software piracy case in Switzerland. He explained that his professional needs made him pay attention to this story because court decisions about digital media cases may affect his work at the university.

R19, a political science student, was routinely checking a list of news sites when he came upon a news story at the *Christian Science Monitor* site about how China was handling swine flu cases. He explained that as a future political scientist he was naturally interested in any topics related to democracy in China.

### Values and Beliefs

Three respondents mentioned that the news stories they incidentally found related to their personal values. While browsing *The New York Times* site during his class, R3, a 19-year-old journalism student, was excited to notice a headline about gay marriage. He explained that this story caught his attention because he is a civil libertarian who believes that gay marriage would be the next "battle of civil liberties in this country."

While checking her email, R12 was incidentally exposed to a news story about President Obama's selection of the nominee for the U.S. Court of Appeals. She noticed the headline of the story in an email from NewsMatch.com because the candidate was viewed as extremely liberal, with his views on issues such as abortion diverging severely from her own conservative stance. She was worried that the nominated judge's votes could affect the environment in which her children will be growing up.

R13 noticed a headline about an interview with a prominent advocate of establishment of local currencies. This headline appeared on the blog feed from his Google Reader news service and attracted his attention because he is involved in a project to promote the idea of using a local currency in order to survive without relying on the U.S. dollar and the national financial infrastructure.

### Sense of Community

A few respondents reported that they came across news stories related to communities where they used to live. One such example is R15, who noticed the headline and links to news stories about the first anniversary of an earthquake in China while browsing the news on Next China, a news site for Chinese people living abroad. She said she paid attention to this story because she cares about people in her home country and wanted to know what was happening.

### Bizarre News

In a few cases, respondents noted that the oddity or bizarreness of a story caught their attention and led them to experience IEON. R17 said she came across a news story about Susan Boyle (a Scottish singer who came to international public attention when she appeared as a contestant on the British reality TV program *Britain's Got Talent*) at the Yahoo! homepage. She had heard about this story from a friend two days earlier and was curious about it.

While reading news at themorningnews.com, R10 was incidentally exposed to a news story about a South African president who was a polygamist. While polygamy is culturally acceptable in the South African or Zulu tribe, this is not a common behavior among the leaders of the industrialized world, which drew the attention of R10 to the story. During the think-aloud session, he demonstrated how he encountered this story and showed the exact headline: "Fascinating Consideration of Wife Hierarchy: South Africa Will Have a Polygamist President."

## 5.2.2 STOPPING

In the IE model, Stopping follows Noticing. It is a point when a person interrupts the activity that was under way to devote attention to the information that was encountered. The questions that guided our exploration here are as follows: How does this step presents itself in IEON? What happens when somebody notices certain headlines or other trigger elements?

All respondents reported that they stopped to read news stories or watch video stories they encountered immediately after they noticed interesting (or trigger) headlines. A number of factors appear to determine whether a user immediately stopped the primary activity to read the encountered news stories: (1) importance, immediacy, and relevance of the encountered story; (2) surprising nature of the encountered news story; (3) immediate emotional response when users noticed a trigger headline (strong positive or negative emotions affect users' next actions in IEON and the news reading process); (4) context of experiencing IEON (workplace, character of foreground task when user was exposed incidentally to news stories, availability of time); and (5) personality or individual differences. Depending on these factors, news readers use different strategies in their IEON experience: stopping immediately to read the encountered story, capturing stories for future reading, and/or sharing.

## 5.2.3 READING

Respondents used various strategies when reading the encountered news stories. This process involved reading (the encountered news stories, other related stories, comments), watching news videos, evaluating (finding the stories missed, checking the archive of the newspaper, checking accuracy/credibility/trustworthiness of the story by looking at other sources for coverage of the same story), and getting outcomes, even if they were not immediately visible. Reading encountered news stories also often led respondents to more IEON.

The most commonly reported action following stopping is to read news stories or watch video stories that were encountered immediately after noticing interesting news headlines. R5 stated that he was shocked to encounter a news story about a potential takeover of the company that is in charge of software he uses for his work. He stopped the process of checking email and not only read the encountered story but also posted a question to the discussion board. He described the situation as "an emergency" and said "it was a huge story and it took everyone by surprise." This "bombshell" interrupted his workday.

Several respondents stated that they examine the accuracy, credibility, and trustworthiness of encountered news stories. R16 said that she reads Digg.com comments to check if there is any spin on news stories. She explained that comments often point out biases in stories, offering additional links. R16 shared she believes "in the wisdom of crowds" more than she believes "in the wisdom of a single journalist." She goes through the comments quickly to see if there's anything that jumps out at her. R5 also said he reads the comments below the story to get different viewpoints on the incidentally exposed news story. He stressed that the comments are often "more informing than the information that is given" in the story.

R4 said that he looks at the name of the news sources and makes judgments about trustworthiness, saying he will "pretty much trust right away, at least for basic facts," a name he can recognize or has prior experience with, including the big newspapers. However, he also said that he trusts stories on Boing Boing much more than the big sites because they tend to correct themselves very noticeably when they are wrong.

R18 explained that her "perception of the reliability of the site that it is on, more so than anything else" helps her determine the credibility of the news story she incidentally comes across. She said she has "more faith" in the website of "an academic institution" in "whatever they tell." For other sites, she looks for bias and whether she has "a track record of them seeming reliable."

### 5.2.4   CAPTURING

Our findings indicate that capturing may be a multi-layer process, involving extraction of useful information from the encountered news stories, saving the actual story for future reading, or finding a way to save it in order to read it immediately.

A few respondents reported that they captured important information such as phone numbers and URLs from encountered news stories. For example, R1 wrote down the phone number from the story that she came across in a local newspaper and then contacted and met the subject of the article. The majority of the respondents, however, stated that they did not capture or save the encountered news stories. R4 explained that he did not bookmark a news story about a trial in Europe because it did not directly affect him enough to reference it in the future or affect anyone else that he needed to send it to. R16 said he does not capture the news stories but tries to remember them.

Those respondents who did capture encountered news stories presented different strategies to do so, depending on the nature of the news stories and their relevance. We found two different paths for how capturing happens: from the Reading step or from the Stopping step. While some respondents captured the encountered news story after reading it, others reported that they do not actually stop to read the encountered news stories immediately after they notice them. Instead, they use different strategies to capture the encountered stories to read later, such as opening new tabs to maintain the flow of their primary activity or by saving the story for future reading (bookmarking in browser, marking as "read" in Google News Reader, using Twitter or Facebook, sending email, and so forth).

Think-aloud sessions during the interviews revealed that opening new tabs in web browsers was the most prominent behavior in the IEON process. After noticing interesting stories, many respondents reported that they opened new tabs to keep incidentally exposed news stories and continued the process of news browsing without interruption. R4 said he right-clicked the mouse to open a new tab to keep an incidentally exposed news story. He opened several tabs with links from the full article in his browser to read later and then continued reading through the rest of the blog. He explained that he opens five or six tabs with links that he wants to further explore and continues reading for other things he finds interesting so that his news-finding task can continue without interruption. After finding all the information of interest to him, he starts reading stories and closes tabs for any story that is not interesting. R5 similarly noted he opens tabs to save a story for later and returns to his work-related task. R16 said she opens new tabs to read interesting encountered news stories to make it easier to go back to what she was doing before.

Saving encountered news stories for future reading was an important task for many respondents during their IEON experiences. Strategies for saving stories included bookmarking in their browsers or in social bookmarking (Delicious), sending through email, sharing on Twitter, and marking as "read" in Google News Reader. R4 shared that he uses Google Tool Bar and the Google Bookmarks on his computer "throughout the day" to save news sources and interesting stories for future reading because he does not have much time to read everything he is interested in during his office hours. He said he uses his Delicious account to save his "technology-related" bookmarks separately from the information related to his personal interests so that he can hand them out to people at work. R10 likewise keeps "unusual" or "interesting" stories for future reading. He said he does not print out the stories but instead, as did several others, emails the links to news stories to his personal email. R12 said that she saves the interesting news stories in Google News Reader for the "next time" she goes back to "browse through all of the news things...found earlier."

Some respondents stated that posting the link on Facebook or Twitter helped them find the encountered news stories later for reading. R13 said he uses the "favorite" button in Twitter to save the stories for future reading. In case of one critical incident story, R13 noted that he did not save a copy of the encountered news story about local currencies, because he sent it to his friend on Facebook, thus "leaving a trail" to ensure "important things get saved, sort of." The links to the stories related to his interests and hobbies found during his working day are saved for after work. For example, he said he saved a six-page interview with Barack Obama and read it on his iPhone while "waiting for somebody to show up." R4 marks the interesting news stories in his Google News Reader as "read" for future reading if he is not using his own computer, and likes that Google News Reader automatically color codes stories that he scrolls through to read.

## 5.2.5    SHARING

Sharing the encountered news stories with others was a prominent behavior in IEON. Erdelez and Rioux (2000) found that the sharing of encountered information with others is a prominent behavior on the Internet; even "short sessions" on websites could trigger IE experiences that "result in useful information for both users themselves and for people they know" (p. 229). Ten of our respondents shared encountered news stories, using different strategies: sending email, clicking on Share buttons in news sites, posting links to Facebook and other social networking sites, posting questions on online discussion forums, and making personal communications about the encountered story.

Many respondents stated that they send emails with links to encountered news stories to their family members, colleagues, and friends. R13 sent the link to a video story he encountered to several friends "so that they could watch it and probably in the future we'll talk about that." When R14 encounters something interesting, she copies it "real quick" and sends it off to someone.

A few respondents shared news they found incidentally with friends or spouses in person or over the phone. R12 stated that she made a mental note to herself about the incidentally exposed news story on the judicial nomination and shared about the story with her husband later. When R7 read the encountered news story about the captain who was rescued from Somali pirates by Navy Seals, she called her husband and told him about the story. She saved the story about the captain at her home so that her husband could read it later. During the think-aloud session, she encountered a news story about the lockdown of a local school. She said she would share this story with her husband and put this story on their prayer list.

Many respondents described sharing encountered news stories via social networking sites and Twitter. R3 said that two-thirds of his tweets have a link to news stories that he regards as important, and just under half of his Facebook status updates reflect his reactions to important news stories. He used the options to Share or Share via Facebook to share, for example, a story about gay marriage he happened to stumble upon on *The New York Times* site. R16 stated that she puts a link on Facebook if she thinks a news article is interesting. She shares only certain stories when she wants to "evangelize" something. For example, having stumbled upon an article about a shooting and the associated comments, she found a link to an article with video of a police officer demonstrating the differences among different types of guns. Concerned about the many "misunderstandings" about gun issues, she posted a link to this story on Facebook because it "totally blew her mind."

### 5.2.6 RETURNING/WANDERING OFF

In order to investigate the Returning step, we examined whether respondents came back to the initial website where they were exposed to certain news stories incidentally. If people return to these initial websites after they pursue the news stories they come across, then how do they know where to return? What factors affect their decision to return or wander off?

Our analysis of interview data about general IEON behavior indicates that users do not always return to the original task or website where they experience IEON. The following factors affect their decisions: nature of the primary activity (initial purpose, intention), time availability, time of day, nature of the encountered news story, content of the initial website, and social needs to converse about the encountered news story.

Several respondents noted their decision to return or wander off depends on the nature of the encountered news story, including its topic, relevance, impact, importance, complexity, and scope. R8 said that he rarely returns to the previous website, and instead, if the story has a direct impact on him, he tends to go to a different section of the new site to seek more information. For R7, the decision to return to the primary activity or place where she first came across the news depends on her purpose. If her goal is to look at classified ads, she returns to her initial task until she finds what she was looking for. When she works on a homework assignment, she would return to complete it. However, if she was browsing the Internet to see what catches her attention, she would keep on wandering. The content of the initial site where she encounters online news affects her decision in that if she gets enough information and feels done, she won't go back to that page after wandering away from it; if, however, there is something more and she wants to "follow all the way through," she will return to the page.

## Returning

The Returning step appeared to be more defined and easy to recall for respondents. In 18 out of 20 cases, respondents returned to what they were doing when they encountered news stories. In seven cases, respondents encountered news from email and then returned to checking email; ten respondents stated that they returned to the online news site where they were exposed to news initially. In three cases, respondents switched from reading news to a non-news activity.

Ten respondents reported that they continued reading more news stories on the same site after their IEON experience. After encountering a synopsis about the verdict in the software piracy case in Switzerland, R4 read the full story and then continued reading through the rest of the site. Upon reading a story about the first anniversary of an earthquake in China, R15 closed the tab and came back to the Next China news website, where she had found the news story. R16 went back to the main page on Digg.com and continued browsing for more news stories once she finished reading the encountered news story about Sarah Palin and the comments to the story. R11 read the encountered story about H1N1 and went back to CNN.com, but nothing more interested her on the site and she closed out the page.

Two respondents reported that they went to different sites after their IEON experiences during news browsing. After sharing the encountered news story about gay marriage in Iowa, R3 did not return to *The New York Times* site, but he went to the *Washington Post* and *Des Moines Register*. This was a part of his daily news reading habits, which involved switching through bookmarks of a dozen news sources. After encountering a news story at *The Christian Science Monitor* site about how the Chinese government was handling swine flu cases, R19 said he did not read the entire article, but he went to another website about comic books.

Ten respondents reported that they returned to a non-news-related task/activity after they were exposed to news incidentally. After reading a story about Oracle software and exploring more about the merger of two companies, R5 went back to checking his email. R7 reported that she went back to the classified section of the local newspaper to continue looking for furniture. R12 went back to her emails after reading a news story about a newly nominated judge. R17 returned to her email after she read a news story about Susan Boyle on Yahoo! After reading a story about the student with swine flu, R18 returned to her work. Upon reading a news story about a divorce controversy from the TV reality-show *John and Kate Plus 8* at the MSN site, R20 continued her Google search on the topic of dyslexia.

Three respondents reported that they returned to their work after they experienced IEON. After reading the news story about a South African president that he encountered at themorningnews.com during his break, which lasted "somewhere between five and seven minutes," R10 felt satisfied he had read something interesting, but not interesting enough to devote it additional attention. He therefore went back to his work to be more productive.

When R13 encountered a news story about Douglas Rushkoff during his short recess from work, he started watching the video interview on YouTube, but he was not able to watch the full video immediately. He said that this video was rather long, consisting of five parts, each about eight minutes. R13 watched a video for 10 minutes, shared the story with his friends on Facebook, and went back to what he was doing for his work. Because this story was very interesting, he went back to the video a couple of times throughout the day to finish it, and eventually watched the whole thing.

### Wandering Off

Many people often do not return to the initial location where they encountered news. Instead, they wander off or switch to an intentional search for different information following their IEON experience.

R6 said his decision of returning or wandering off depends on the scope of the news story and his social needs to converse about this news. If the encountered news is "a huge story," he "may see…what other people are saying," whereas for news "not a lot of people may be talking about," he "won't really look into other pieces." If the topic is "a huge thing," he may even visit Wikipedia and "look it up" to get "general information about it." Going to Wikipedia might cause him to explore further the topic of the encountered news story, going "off on a lot of tangents." R8 reported that he wanders off more than he would like to admit. He said that he "goofs around" too much on the Internet thinking that he is going to learn something. He noted that if the story is of direct relevance to him, he tends to look for more information. R9 also admitted that she wanders off in most cases because she is overwhelmed with a "barrage of information that is coming all the time." She accused our "culture of attention deficit disorder" of making it "hard to filter and focus." R14 likewise said her decision to wander off at work "depends" on time available and whether she is bored. Two respondents said they usually return to the primary activity. R18 said that, in most cases, she returns to the original task of checking email after she is exposed to news incidentally. Especially if the trigger was not the last thing that she needed to open in her inbox, she goes back to finish checking emails.

R19 explained that he does not pursue the news stories he accidentally runs into because he is concerned about losing focus and spending hours without accomplishing anything. He commented that the news stories he encounters are not very important to him because they confirm facts or merely look into topics from another perspective. He described some news stories, such as celebrity news, he runs across as trivial.

CHAPTER 6

# Conceptual Framework of IEON

## 6.1 DEFINITION OF IEON

Our findings indicate that IEON is a complex behavior, deeply embedded in the daily news consumption habits of individuals. With the numerous technological advancements in news delivery, people have much more flexible and rich media environments, as compared to the traditional media outlets of the past, which follow a pre-determined schedule to disseminate news. Interview respondents stated that they are inundated with media, "soaked in media," "constantly being shot with news," and living in an "attention deficit disorder society," overloaded with news and information. They called the Internet an "interwoven network of news and information." We found that online news consumption behavior, including IEON, is affected by respondents' lifestyle, work, interests/hobbies, access to the Internet, available time, and their emotional feelings. These findings are partially supported by Pentina and Tarafdar (2014). They found that paucity of time and busy lifestyle, as well as general attitude toward the news are the contextual factors affecting online news consumers when they decide on different strategies (e.g., news avoidance, information load adjustment, information complexity handling) to deal with information overload.

To help define IEON, we asked the question, What is IEON from a news consumer's perspective? We found that IEON is a subjective and internal experience that is difficult to observe and determine from outside. Only individuals themselves can decide whether an experience is serendipitous or not. These findings confirm Rubin et al.'s (2011) point that serendipitous experience can only be considered serendipitous upon reflection. An important question to investigate is what influences the perception of IEON. Based on Erdelez's (1997) conceptual definition of IE, we initially defined IEON as the user's memorable experiences of accidental discovery of useful and interesting news when engaged in various activities online. This definition includes the accidental, unintentional, and unexpected nature of the behavior with positive outcomes. Our grounded theory-based data analysis revealed that the intention and memorability of the IEON experience based on encountered content and its outcomes are the potential factors that individuals apply when they think about this behavior. In addition, we found that awareness is another important facet that could enhance the definition of IEON. Based on our research, we propose the IEON conceptual framework depicted in Figure 6.1.

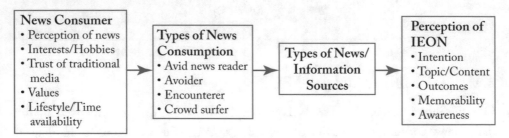

Figure 6.1: Conceptual Framework of IEON.

## 6.2   FACETS OF IEON

*Intention* as a complex factor is used to differentiate what is considered incidental discovery of news. A few respondents felt strongly that the definition of IEON should be restricted to experiences when the intention of the primary activity was not related to news reading. These respondents defined IEON as coming across news when they were doing "something not related to news," such as checking email or visiting social media sites. This definition resembles the perception of IEON in the non-news-reading context presented in our findings. However, those respondents who perceived IEON in the news-browsing context included experiences of coming across unexpected, unusual, or interesting news items while they visited online news sites.

These two types of perceptions of IEON could be explained by the fact that individuals hold different views of news, which in turn affects the ways they consume news and the sources they use. It is apparent from our study that due to the Internet's nature as an information-rich environment, it is becoming complicated to differentiate the types of information and information sources online. Ambiguity and difficulty with the definition of news were visible in the following words used in the definition of news by many respondents: "anything," "whatever," "all," "general."

The four types of news consumers (avid news readers, news avoiders, news encounterers and crowd surfers) show how the potential outcomes of IEON could vary in the diversity, quality, and volume of news users get exposed to. As compared to avid news readers, who mainly consume news from a limited number of news sites affiliated with traditional media, the other three groups of news consumers have more opportunities to be exposed to news from different sources. However, credibility and quality of news from those sources differ, not necessarily with an outcome of the consumer becoming a more informed citizen. The behavior of avid news consumers and news encounterers resembles deliberate news seekers' and incidental news consumers' coping strategies for information overload identified in the Pentina and Tarafdar (2014) study. Deliberate news consumers use goal-directed, intentional strategies to keep up with the major events happening in the world, evaluate different opinions, and make informed decisions, whereas incidental news consumers do not deliberately seek out news on certain topics. Instead, they are rather passively exposed to TV at home, radio in the car, word-of-mouth at work, social media postings by friends, and online news aggregators' and email portals' headlines. Some strategies employed by deliberate news seekers were evident in the news consumption habits of avid news readers: subscription to newsfeeds from news media organizations, creation of portals for personal curation, and possession of a list of online news sites for routine monitoring.

Pentina and Tarafdar's (2014) findings about the avoidance strategies, such as reduction in the number of sources, media, and volume to be exposed to and even avoidance of news altogether, resemble the behavior and news attitude of news avoiders in our study. The reasons for avoiding news due to negatively charged emotional and affective states when reading "sad" news stories are similar to the news avoiders' emotional feelings that we found in our study. The "social legitimacy strategy" (Pentina and Tarafdar, 2014) that relies on others for forming opinions and knowledge to reduce information overload appeared to be a dominant strategy for crowd surfers, who rely on the wisdom of the crowd in their selection of news stories to read.

Our findings indicate that certain outcomes from an IEON experience play an important role in users' perception of it being both memorable and serendipitous. Potential outcomes related to knowledge enhancement might not be obvious immediately after the IEON experience, but emotional responses could be more immediate; other outcomes include gaining knowledge, making personal connections, and changing perspectives. Our findings in regard to knowledge enhancement partially support Makri and Blandford's (2012a) conclusion that the value of the outcome (whether it is knowledge-enhancing, impactful, timely, or time-saving) might become apparent at the time of the serendipitous experience or sometime later.

*Memorability* of the experience due to the nature of encountered news content and its outcomes distinguishes IEON behavior from a habitual news consumption. Respondents were able to describe only those incidents of IEON with significant benefit to them or those cases that led to deep and unforgettable emotional reactions. Additional analysis of study data presented here by Yadamsuren and Heinström

(2011) found that emotions associated with IEON (whether reactions related to the incidental exposure or to the news content they encountered) play a prominent role in the *outcomes* and satisfaction of respondents. Recalling positive experiences could be explained by suggestions from cognitive psychology that the enhancing influence of positive affect on cognition, including openness to information reception and greater levels of aspiration and exploration, may be related to neurotransmitters like dopamine being present in greater quantities at such times (Isen, 2004, p. 430).

Our study also supports the conclusion that serendipitous information experience leads to fortuitous outcomes (McBirnie, 2008; Rubin et al., 2011; Makri and Blandford, 2012b). McBirnie (2008) found that "serendipitous events were not just good; they were seen as extremely exciting and positive, as highlights in the information seeking" (p. 607). Contrary to these studies, however, we found that IEON could cause negative emotional outcomes and reactions to incidentally exposed news if individuals found the news bad and disturbing. In some instances, negative feelings were caused regardless of the content because the readers felt guilty for wasting time or getting distracted from their work.

The respondents presented different levels of *awareness* of IEON in their news consumption. The varying levels of awareness could be explained by the differences among information encounterers. As we mentioned before, many respondents explained that IEON just happens when something catches their attention. Most of them admitted that they did not think about this behavior prior to our interviews. Once their attention was drawn to the behavior, they said that IEON was happening all along and is not anything new. For some of them IEON happens "pretty frequently," but they don't really think about the process of how it happens. These findings could indicate that IEON is a part of the daily news consumption habits of individuals.

We propose to define IEON as a *memorable* experience of a *chance encounter* with news (news *relevant* to an individual's information needs/interest or *surprising news*) while the individual is using the Internet for news browsing or non-news-related online activities, such as checking email or visiting social networking sites. It is hard to separate IEON from daily news consumption habits. This behavior is intertwined with active or purposeful news consumption. These findings are supported by Kim et al. (2013). They found that Internet users' rational election of entertainment and accidental exposure to news take place simultaneously.

## 6.3    PROCESS MODEL OF IEON

Having holistically investigated the IEON process by looking at individual's behavioral, cognitive, and affective elements involved, we propose an IEON Process Model (Figure 6.2), which provides a rich picture of serendipitous news discovery experience from the moment of exposure to the reader's consequential reactions to the content encountered.

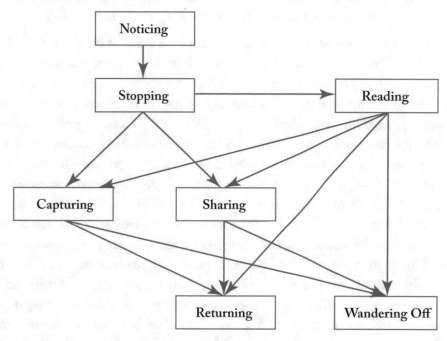

Figure 6.2: IEON Process Model.

According to the model shown in Figure 6.2, the IEON process consists of the following steps:

1. Noticing: User notices news trigger elements in the online environment.

2. Stopping: User diverts attention from the primary activity to the encountered news story and makes a decision about how to pursue further.

3. User chooses one or a combination of three paths:

   a. Reading: User reads the encountered news or watches news videos.

   b. Capturing: User captures the encountered news story (saving it for future reading or temporary capture to keep the flow of reading).

    c. Sharing: User shares the story with other people.

4. User either returns to the primary information activity or wanders off, exploring other information/links:

    a. Returning: User returns to primary information activity.

    b. Wandering off: User does not return to the primary information activity, but instead goes to different activity/task/site.

The steps presented in the model provide a description of the mechanics of this process based on users' behavioral, cognitive, and affective aspects and their response and reactions to the trigger elements for chance encounters. The detailed description of specific behaviors associated with each step of the IEON model and their unique features is provided in Appendix 2. Notably, the IEON process happens very quickly and the steps described in the model can often happen simultaneously, not necessarily following the order presented or involving all steps. In many cases, we saw that several steps, such as Noticing, Stopping, Reading, Sharing, and Capturing, can happen simultaneously. IEON cannot be observed as a single episode, because this behavior can be stretched over time with delays of the main steps involved in the process because of multitasking opportunities online. Many respondents reported that they read news to get a break from what they are doing. A number of respondents stated that they capture/share stories for future reading if they don't have time to read them immediately following their IEON experience. Some respondents noted that they do not capture or share news stories. Others returned to the encountered story several times in order to finish reading it. Moreover, IEON is not limited to Internet activities. The initial exposure (Noticing) can happen through other media channels and information sources (most frequently through personal communication and radio). Participants paid attention to news triggers that they were exposed to in the physical environment sometime earlier, such as listening to the radio in the car or casual talk with friends and colleagues. These findings suggest that IEON cannot be separated from an individual's ELIS behavior. Also, various behaviors associated with each step in the IEON process are indicative of personal information management (Jones, 2007; Whittaker, 2011).

Our findings indicate that individuals pay attention to the trigger elements if they are important, relevant, or interesting to them. Immediacy of the story, such as an outbreak of the swine flu virus, caught the attention of a few respondents because of its importance. In many cases, the reason for paying attention to the trigger elements was related to a respondent's personal and professional information needs. Respondents also paid attention to news headlines because they felt an immediate connection with their values (e.g., gay marriage, local currencies) or were concerned about government's decision-making shaking their values. A few respondents claimed that their caring for their community contributed to their IEON.

One of the most interesting findings from our study was that individuals may experience IEON out of curiosity when they see surprising news stories. Several respondents paid attention to bizarre or odd news stories out of curiosity. Fredin (1997) also identified curiosity as a key element for news browsing and serendipitous discovery. He noted that curiosity is raised by novel, somewhat novel, and surprising or ambiguous stimuli in hypertext news environment. He explained that curiosity involves interconnected aspects of cognition, emotion, and motivation. Rubin et al. (2011) recognized the importance of surprise in serendipitous encounters, concluding that surprise may operate as a cognitive/emotional reaction to the serendipitous encounter or as a trigger for an orienting or noticing response.

In addition to relevance of news stories to consumers' information needs, the initial emotional response seemed to play a vital role in the decision-making of individuals on whether to pursue their IEON behavior, especially at the steps of Noticing and Stopping. Our findings support research recognizing the role of emotions in information behavior (Nahl, 1998; Nahl and Bilal, 2007). Affective filters influence the information acquisition process, for example, which pieces of information we ignore and which we stop to examine (Nahl, 1998). We found that once they notice news stories that are interesting or relevant to them, individuals progress to Reading, a complex process involving many cognitive and affective elements and important for the potential outcomes discussed earlier. Respondents read not only the encountered news stories but also other related stories and comments, to see different perspectives on the topic; as one respondent stated, the comments are often "more informing" than the information in the story. In many cases, they take additional steps to learn more about the topic covered in the encountered news stories by visiting the online archive of news stories and checking the accuracy of the story by visiting other news sources.

During the reading process, individuals share and capture the encountered news stories. Many respondents commented that they share the encountered news stories with their family members, friends, and colleagues to discuss later by sending email, clicking on the Share button in news sites, posting a link to Facebook and other social networking sites, posting a question on online discussion forums, and making personal communications about the encountered story. The prominence of the Sharing step supports Erdelez and Rioux's (2000) conclusions, as detailed in Chapter 2.

Returning was the most complicated step in the IEON process due to individual variability in navigating the web environment. We examined whether respondents came back to the initial website (either online news sites or non-news sites, such as email and social networking sites) where they were exposed to certain news stories incidentally. Our findings indicate that users do not always return to the original task or website where they experience IEON, contradicting Erdelez's (2000) assumption that individuals return to the primary activity after IE. Most of our respondents stated that "it depends" when asked whether they would return to the initial website. The factors affecting respondents' decisions to return to the initial site or wander off by exploring more about the same or other topics include the following: their initial purpose in the primary activity; time availability and time of the day; the interest, importance, impact, complexity, and scope of the encountered news story; the content of the initial website; and social needs to converse about the encountered news story.

We found that mostly negative emotional outcomes, such as wasting time, are associated with wandering off. These negative emotions were expressed as "goofing around," too much on the Internet to "learn" something, and "bouncing around." On the other hand, diversion from the routine work as a result of IEON could bring positive outcomes. Short breaks to wander off or experience IEON helped respondents to be productive and provided a short mental break. There are many factors that affect potential outcomes: news consumption habits, perception of news, personality/individual differences, content of the topic encountered, the way it was encountered, emotions involved with the discovery during and after IEON, and so on. In general, respondents reported satisfaction with their serendipitous news discovery outcomes: learning something new, making new contacts for personal and professional needs, getting emotional satisfaction, and so on. Negative outcomes could also result, due to the nature of encountered news stories or the feeling of wasting time and being distracted. Surprise and serendipity are connected. In many cases, individuals may experience IEON as a result of reading bizarre news.

## 6.4    IEON AND THE PUBLIC SPHERE

An important question remains: Could IEON guarantee the expected outcomes for maintaining or even broadening the public sphere as expected by communication scholars? Our conceptual framework of IEON urges caution in high expectations of serendipitous news discovery as an antidote to get past audience fragmentation issues based on the following points.

First, despite the numerous opportunities to come across news online, citizens may be living in their own information spheres, bubbles, or digital flocks because serendipitous news discovery seems to be taking place within their typical information practice/habit. Their news consumption habit may revolve around a limited number of sources and depend on their perceptions of what is considered news. Our findings indicate that a news consumption habit is highly individualized based on people's interest and hobbies, values, beliefs, lifestyle, trust of traditional media, and perception of news. Online news consumption habits and IEON experiences are based on an individual's perception of news and rational selection of information sources and Facebook friends. Thorson and Wells (2015) argued that exposure to any given message to an individual is defined by the five sets of curating actors: journalists, strategic communicators, individual media users (personal curators), social curation, and algorithmic filters. The four types of news consumers presented in our conceptual framework present totally different information experiences. Avid news readers might be the only group that have a higher chance of being exposed to news from journalistic curation. Their online news consumption might replicate that of the traditional news audience of the past compared to the other three types of news consumers. However, news avoiders, news encounterers, and crowd surfers might have little chance of being exposed to current affairs news produced by professional media. For example, news encounterers, who rely on IEON to be informed about news events, may not check traditional media sources and might miss important news and issues unless they pop up in their information sphere at Yahoo! or on social media sites.

Second, the whole online information experience of individuals could affect their IEON experience because of various search engine and application algorithms. Tufecki (2014) cautioned about the power of "computational politics" fundamentally reshaping the public sphere (Habermas, 1989). She wrote about the danger of "opaque and black-box" algorithms that are hidden from ordinary citizens with regard to content visibility, data sharing, and many other features of political decision-making and other consequences. These algorithms determine the visibility of content and can be changed at will, with enormous consequences for political speech. Pariser (2011) brought to our attention the danger of a "filter bubble" formed by invisible algorithms offering individuals news and information that mainly confirm their existing beliefs, based on past experience and information needs. Thorson and Wells (2015) cautioned that increased automated personalization could extend the gap between the political information-rich and the political information-poor, and between the political left and right. Bakshy et al. (2015) found that how much crosscutting ideological content individuals encounter on Facebook depends on their social network of friends, the news feed population algorithm, and an individual's own selection. Nikolov et al. (2015) studied the relationship between the diversity of information sources experienced by users at both the collective and individual levels in Twitter posts and search logs. They found that the diversity of information and news traffic reached through social media is significantly lower than the nature of content that individuals find through a search and interpersonal communication. The authors caution about the increased danger of reinforcing a collective filter bubble via social media. Trigger elements for IEON (most read, most emailed, most popular, most blogged, highly rated, comments, and so on) illustrate the nature of the complexity of the online information environment ruled by various algorithms. Depending on the intention behind these algorithms, individuals may have little power over what content they will come across in a networked world and how they might take potential advantage of being exposed to different viewpoints as is expected from political and mass communication research.

Third, news consumers' personal interest in certain topics, ideological viewpoints, and values play a huge role in what will catch their eye on the Internet and in the outcomes of IEON. However, IEON does not guarantee that citizens will be exposed to current affairs news, crosscutting information (Mutz, 2006), and different perspectives on certain issues. Mitchell et al, (2013) finds that Facebook news consumers get news they agree with, not necessarily opposing their viewpoints. In addition, many people prefer entertainment over news. Several studies show that entertainment use of the Internet may have a negative impact on the public's political knowledge and engagement, whereas news consumption may have a positive effect (Prior, 2005; Scheufele and Nisbet, 2002). Pentina and Tarafdar (2014) argue that people who like entertainment might abandon or ignore news and information when they stumble upon news inadvertently, whereas those people who prefer news might take advantage of incidental news exposure, such as mobilizing information, when they accidently encounter information about politics.

# CHAPTER 7

# Implications and Future Directions

## 7.1 IMPLICATIONS FOR THE MEDIA INDUSTRY

The complexity of the modern information environment wired with abundant and competing online news services and entertainment options challenges media to fulfill its duty to keep the public informed about the major issues facing society. The media industry struggles with how to keep and expand target audiences, how to engage consumers who are more interested in awareness of their friends' social lives than of today's pressing issues.

This study presented in this book lays out a conceptual framework that could help media professionals to understand serendipitous news discovery from individuals' holistic experiences of news consumption in their daily lives. Our findings demonstrate that IEON is a promising behavior to encourage in the online environment because respondents like to be exposed to news that enhances their knowledge and deepens their curiosity. However, this conclusion is tempered by the possibility that news consumers could be following their own perceived definition of news, and, in some cases, the content of news may be favored for purely entertainment value (or for bizarreness or for surprise and curiosity), not necessarily associated with the benefits of knowledge enhancement or crosscutting information as expected by communication scholars.

The IEON conceptual framework provides the initial insights about which factors need to be considered to induce serendipitous news encounters, where media organizations should place their news stories to invite clicks, and how to enter the information/news sphere of individuals as a part of their news consumption habits. Media organizations need to abandon the old tradition of treating news consumers as a whole audience and instead focus on news consumers' individual behaviors and develop unique strategies to reach the different types of news consumers identified by the study discussed here. The findings of this study suggest that news media organizations need to develop innovative policy and creative strategies to compete with various algorithms controlling information flows to citizens to keep them informed and to promote the diversity of ideas in the public sphere. How can news organizations compete and break invisible algorithms to reduce filter bubble effects and guard their duty to keep the public informed? News organizations need to actively seek better models to establish and run their own accounts on social media or other sites to offer their readers more diverse exposure to various sources offering relevant information.

The IEON Process Model offers a rich picture of the serendipitous news discovery experience, from the moment of exposure to the reader's subsequent reactions to the encountered content. This process model provides a rich description of an IEON episode: trigger elements for serendipity, individual characteristics of news consumers, the underlying information needs that expose them to news online, the nature of news they find, and potential outcomes from this experience. The detailed descriptions of the decision-making reasons for each step involved in the IEON process could help news designers and writers to develop innovative storytelling and design ideas to catch news consumers' attention and take advantage of the high likelihood of citizens to come across news while they are doing various activities online. For example, the Noticing step could suggest the importance of providing more consideration to the writing of eye-catching headlines that grab the attention of readers in the midst of their multitasking activities in information-overloaded environments. The Returning step provides some insights into conditions that bring the news consumers back to the site after experiencing IEON.

## 7.2   METHODOLOGICAL IMPLICATIONS

This study employed a constructivist approach to identify the multiple realities of the phenomena of serendipitous news discovery perceived by individuals, using the active interview technique to construct the meaning of this ambiguous behavior. The mixed method was used to investigate the complex behaviors involved in serendipitous news discovery, and all the techniques were helpful in exploring online news reading behavior. We attempted to capture unobservable cognitive behavior with self-reported and retrospective thinking during interviews about critical incidents. Think-aloud sessions captured many detailed behaviors that respondents undertook during online news reading. Nonetheless, respondents rarely volunteered during think-aloud sessions that they were exposed to news incidentally. Think-aloud sessions seemed to be limited to capturing IEON when the respondents were interviewed in a controlled environment.

The subjective, memorability-based nature of this behavior seems to be one of the biggest challenges to investigating serendipity in information behavior, given the varying perceptions of what is considered news by different individuals. Given the demonstrated complexity of investigating serendipitous news discovery, we call for new methods. Most research on IEON in mass communication rely on surveys, do not capture the nuances and complexity of this behavior. Survey questions about serendipitous news discovery may not elicit the right responses from news consumers. Mitchelstein and Boczkowski (2010) also called for an integrative approach using mixed methods to better understand the "multiple relevant dimensions" of online news consumption. They suggested that research on news consumption should inquire into when, where, how, and under what conditions this happens—and does not happen—and its consequences for issues such as displacement, complementarity, and civic participation. We urge including among the mixed method approaches objective measurements, such as eye-tracking and psycho-physiological measurements; naturalistic approaches to investigate IEON in news consumers' daily information habits, including tracking their behavior unobtrusively; and using data-mining tools to analyze behavioral data.

## 7.3 FUTURE RESEARCH

Compared to previous research on serendipitous news discovery, which has primarily relied on survey research, this study takes a novel methodological approach; it looks into individuals' perceptions of how they come across news unintentionally in their daily information practice. In interpreting the findings and implications of this study, several caveats should be taken into consideration. Because of the exploratory nature of the study, the respondents' online news reading behavior and IEON are not generalizable beyond the study sample. Selection of the study respondents relied on purposeful sampling and recruitment of participants through the website of a local newspaper affiliated with one of the most prestigious journalism schools in the country. This strategy may have limited the study sample to a group of highly educated, professionally oriented, and predominantly Caucasian respondents. Moreover, the findings of this study are limited to the notion of a libertarian theory of the press (Siebert et al., 1963). Yin (2008) called for a new paradigm of press theories to address global media systems taking into account both Western and Eastern philosophies and cultural values, in addition to the political control of media and the concept of freedom. Citizens in various countries have different news consumption habits based on their press systems, freedom of expression, cultural values, and technology penetration. All these factors in turn could affect what IEON is perceived as and how it occurs through a global perspective. Therefore, future studies should test and refine the conceptual and process models developed in this study through the investigation of IEON in other countries.

As qualitative data collection did not take place on participants' own computers but on research laboratory computers, respondents were not able to explain their news reading behavior in a natural context. While most of them did not experience difficulties with computer setup, several were not able to demonstrate the specific configurations of their web browsers and any customized tools they rely on for online news reading. This problem should be taken into account in future studies on the information behavior of online news readers.

The conceptual framework of IEON from our research opens the possibility of further exploration of this emerging news consumption behavior and its consequences on the individual and social level. Future research needs to investigate and measure who is most likely experiencing IEON and what types of activities are more likely to expose individuals to news in the constantly changing information world. The increasing number of studies on IEON has been focused on social media as a potential environment (Kim et al., 2013; Mitchell et al., 2013; Pentina and Tarafdar, 2014; Nikolov et al., 2015; Bode, 2016). Except for a few studies, however, there is not much research examining other types of online activities where individuals can experience IEON. Kim et al. (2013) examined IEON in search engines, portal sites, forums or listservs, blogs, and social networking sites. Yadamsuren (2013) conducted experimental research to induce IEON in social game environment applying Erdelez's (2004) model of IE. The game presented a constantly updated stream of local news stories within a gaming environment and captured the time-stamped moments of clicking on those stories as an indication of IEON. This study demonstrated the potential of using a gaming environment for the serendipitous discovery of news.

More detailed research is needed to investigate the IEON experiences of the four types of news consumers identified in the IEON conceptual framework. Future studies should examine potential outcomes from IEON; whether those experiences have helped readers to reach crosscutting information, opposing viewpoints, or new perspectives; and how IEON behavior is different on mobile devices or continues when users switch among multiple devices.

# APPENDIX 1

## Demographics of Interview Respondents

| Interview code | Sex | Age | Ethnicity | Occupation | Major/Field |
|---|---|---|---|---|---|
| R1 | F | 29 | Indian | Homemaker | Innovation and design |
| R2 | F | 54 | African American | Administrative assistant at a bank | Finance |
| R3 | M | 19 | White | Undergraduate student | Journalism |
| R4 | M | 28 | White | Programmer | Computer/ Technology |
| R5 | M | 32 | White | Project coordinator | Educational technology |
| R6 | M | 26 | White | Doctoral student | Educational technology |
| R7 | F | 41 | White | Prevention technician at an insurance company | Business |
| R8 | M | 38 | White | Public school consultant at a university program | Education |
| R9 | F | 31 | White | Program coordinator at a university | Library science |
| R10 | M | 29 | White | Government officer (land use planner) | Public administration |
| R11 | F | 57 | White | Librarian at a public university | Library science |
| R12 | F | 47 | White | Educator for a public school | Education |
| R13 | M | 25 | White | Web developer | Computer science |

| R14 | F | 28 | White | Office support staff | Education |
| R15 | F | 26 | Asian | Graduate student | Educational technology |
| R16 | F | 34 | White | Graduate student | Education |
| R17 | F | 25 | Asian | Graduate student | Educational technology |
| R18 | F | 38 | White | Assistant professor | Medicine |
| R19 | M | 27 | White | Graduate student | Political science |
| R20 | F | 53 | White | Facilitator for a dyslexia and autism program | Education and horticulture |

# APPENDIX 2

# Description of IEON Process Steps

| Steps | Behavioral | Cognitive | Affective |
|-------|-----------|-----------|-----------|
| Noticing | Noticing the trigger elements (perceptual visual experience) | Quick examination of the relevance and importance of the news story based on information needs: <br>• Immediacy of the story/Follow-up needs <br>• Personal relevance <br>• Professional needs <br>• Values and beliefs <br>• Sense of community <br>• Bizarre news | Initial emotional response (strong positive and negative emotions) plays important role in decision-making to pursue IEON or not |
| Stopping | • Click on a story <br>• Follow link <br>• Open new tabs <br>• Right click on window to put story behind | Diverts attention from primary activity to the encountered news story and makes decision about how to pursue further: <br>• Reading <br>• Capturing stories for future reading <br>• Sharing | Strong emotions (excitement, trepidation, etc.) |

| Reading | • Reading comments below the story<br>• Reading other related stories<br>• Finding and reading the stories missed<br>• Checking the archive of the newspaper<br>• Checking other sources for coverage of same story<br>• Getting important information/facts from the story<br>• Watching news video | • Checking accuracy/credibility/trustworthiness of the story by checking other sources for coverage of same story<br>• Gaining knowledge from reading<br>• Changing mind/perspectives based on reading<br>• Making personal connection with the story (events and people described)<br>• Deciding to read more on the topic | Emotional reactions related to IEON (Yadamsuren and Heinström, 2011):<br>• Surveillance<br>• Personal identity (*Discovery, value reinforcement, reassurance, negative feelings related to identification*)<br>• Personal relationships (*Social empowerment related to current issues, increased understanding of others with another background, empathy*)<br>• Diversion<br>• Negative feelings (*Negative news content, feeling of distrus, being distracted, losing focus, wasting of time, lacking control*)<br>• Mixed feelings |
| Capturing | • Get important facts from story<br>• Open new tabs<br>• Save for future reading (bookmark, mark as unread)<br>• Posting on Facebook, Twitter, and other social media | • Quick judgment about time availability<br>• Thinking about future information needs<br>• Thinking about needs of others (family members, friends, colleagues) | Emotional reactions related to the incidental exposure and reactions related to the news content encountered |

| Sharing | • Send email<br>• Click on Share button<br>• Post link on social media (e.g., Facebook)<br>• Post question on discussion forums<br>• Personal communication | • Decision-making: whether to share or not<br>• Thinking about own needs and needs of other people<br>• Thinking about social needs to converse and discuss later | Emotional reactions related to the incidental exposure and reactions related to the news content encountered |
|---|---|---|---|
| Returning | • Continue news browsing<br>• Return to same story, page, location<br>• Go to different section of the initial website<br>• Go to different news site<br>• Closing tabs | Quick decision-making, judging (*It Depends factors*):<br>• Nature of their primary activity (initial purpose, intention)<br>• Time availability<br>• Time of day<br>• Nature of the encountered news story (interest, importance, impact, complexity, scope)<br>• Content of the initial website where they encountered news<br>• Social needs to converse about the encountered news story | • Diversion<br>• Negative feelings (*Negative news content, feeling of being distracted, losing focus, wasting of time, distrust, feeling of lack of control*)<br>• Mixed feelings |

| Wandering off | • Switch to intentional search to find more information<br>• Explore more about the encountered news | Quick decision-making judging (*It Depends factors*):<br>• Nature of their primary activity (initial purpose, intention)<br>• Time availability<br>• Time of day<br>• Nature of the encountered news story (interest, importance, impact, complexity, scope)<br>• Content of the initial website where they encountered news<br>• Social needs to converse about the encountered news story | • Feeling of being distracted, losing focus, wasting time, lacking control<br>• Mixed feelings |

# Bibliography

André, P., Teevan, J., and Dumais, S.T. (2009). From x-rays to silly putty via Uranus: serendipity and its role in web search. Paper presented at the the *27th International Conference on Human Factors in Computing Systems*, Boston, MA, April 4–9, 2009. DOI: 10.1145/1518701.1519009. 11

Bakshy, E., Messing, S., and Adamic, L.A. (2015). Exposure to ideologically diverse news and opinion on Facebook. *Science*, 348 (6239), 1130–1132. DOI: 10.1126/science.aaa1160. 51

Barwise, T. P., Ehrenberg, A.S.C., and Goodhardt, G. J. (1982). Glued to the box. *Journal of Communication*, 32(4), 22–29. DOI: 10.1111/j.1460-2466.1982. tb02515.x. 5

Baum, M.A. (2002). Sex, lies, and war: How soft news brings foreign policy to the inattentive public. *The American Political Science Review*, 96, 91–109. DOI: 10.1017=S0003055402004252. 8

Baum, M.A. and Jamison, A.S. (2006). The Oprah effect: How soft news helps inattentive citizens vote consistently. *The Journal of Politics*, 68, 946–959. DOI: 10.1111=j.1468-2508.2006.00482.x. 8

Brians, C.L. and Wattenberg, M.P. (1996). Campaign issue knowledge and salience: Comparing reception from TV commercials, TV news and newspapers. *American Journal of Political Science*, 40, 172–193. DOI: 10.2307=2111699. 8

Bode, L. (2016). Political news in the news feed: Learning politics from social media. *Mass Communication and Society*, 19(1), 24–48. DOI: 10.1080/15205436.2015.1045149. 56

Case, D. (2002). *Looking for Information: A Survey of Research on Information Seeking, Needs, and Behavior*. New York: Academic Press. 10

Corbin, J.M. and Strauss, A.L. (2008). *Basics of Qualitative Research: Techniques and Procedures for Developing Grounded Theory* (3rd ed.). Los Angeles, CA: Sage Publications. DOI: 10.4135/9781452230153. 20

Creswell, J.W. and Clark, V.L.P. (2007). *Designing and Conducting Mixed Methods Research*. Thousand Oaks, CA: Sage Publications. 17

Cunha, M.P., Clegg, S.R., and Mendonça, S. (2010). On serendipity and organizing. *European Management Journal*, 28(5), 319–330. DOI: 10.1016/j.emj.2010.07.001. 11

Dahl, R.A. (1989). *Democracy and Its Critics*. New Haven, CT: Yale University Press. 1

Delli Carpini, M.X., and Keeter, S. (1996). *What Americans Know about Politics and Why It Matters*. New Haven, CT: Yale University Press. 1

Dey, I. (1999). *Grounding Grounded Theory: Guidelines for Qualitative Inquiry*. San Diego: Academic Press. DOI: 10.1016/b978-012214640-4/50011-5. 18

Donohew, R.L., Nair, M., and Finn, S. (1984). Automaticity, arousal, and information exposure. In R. N. Bostrom (Ed.), *Communication Yearbook* (Vol. 8, pp. 267–284). Beverly Hills, CA: Sage Publications. DOI: 10.1080/23808985.1984.11678578. 6

Downs, A. (1957). *An Economic Theory of Democracy*. New York: Harper. 8

Erdelez, S. (1995). Information Encountering: An Exploration beyond Information Seeking. Unpublished Doctoral dissertation. Syracuse University. 19

Erdelez, S. (1997). Information encountering: A conceptual framework for accidental information discovery. In P. Vakkari, R. Savolainen, and B. Dervin (Eds.), *Information Seeking in Context: Proceedings of an International Conference on Research in Information Needs, Seeking and Use in Different Contexts* (pp. 412–421): London: Taylor Graham. 2, 11, 12, 13, 15, 18, 43

Erdelez, S. (2000). Toward understanding information encountering on the web. *Proceedings of the 63rd Annual Meeting of the American Society for Information Science* (pp. 363–371). Medford, NJ: Information Today. 2, 3, 13, 14, 15, 31, 50

Erdelez, S., and Rioux, K. (2000). Sharing information encountered for others on the web. In L. Höglund and T. D. Wilson (Eds.), *The New Review of Information Behaviour Research* (Vol. 1, pp. 219–223). Cambridge, England: Taylor Graham. 12, 13, 38, 49

Erdelez, S. (2004). Investigation of information encountering in the controlled research environment. *Information Processing and Management*, 40(6), 1013–1025. DOI: 10.1016/j.ipm.2004.02.002. 11, 13, 14, 15, 56

Erdelez, S. (2005). Information Encountering. In K. E. Fisher, S. Erdelez and L. McKechnie (Eds.), *Theories of Information Behavior* (pp. 179–185). Medford, New Jersey: Information Today. 11

Erdelez, S. and Makri, S. (2011). Introduction to the thematic issue on opportunistic discovery of information. *Information Research*, 16(3). Available at http://InformationR.net/ir/16-3/odiintro.html. 11

Feldman, L. and Young, D.G. (2008). Late-night comedy as a gateway to traditional news: An analysis of time trends in news attention among late-night comedy viewers during the 2004 presidential primaries. *Political Communication*, 25, 401–422. DOI: 10.1080/10584600802427013. 8

Flanagan, J.C. (1954). The critical incident technique. *Psychological Bulletin*, 51(4), 327-358. DOI: 10.1037/h0061470. 18, 19

Fredin, E. (1997). Rethinking the news story for the Internet: Hyperstory prototypes and a model of the user. *Journalism and Mass Communication Monographs*, 163, 1–47. 49

Glaser, B.G. and Strauss, A.L. (1967). *The Discovery of Grounded Theory: Strategies for Qualitative Research*. Chicago: Aldine Pub. Co. 18

Habermas, J. (1989). *The Structural Transformation of the Public Sphere: An Inquiry into a Category of Bourgeois Society*. Cambridge, Mass: MIT Press. 1, 51

Heinström, J. (2006). Psychological factors behind incidental information acquisition. *Library and Information Science Research*, 28(4), 579–594. DOI: 10.1016/j.lisr.2006.03.022. 11

Holstein, J.A. and Gubrium, J.F. (1995). *The Active Interview*. Thousand Oaks, CA: Sage Publications. DOI: 10.4135/9781412986120. 3, 19

Horna, J. (1988). The mass media as leisure: A Western-Canadian case. *Society and Leisure*, 11(2), 283–301. DOI: 10.1080/07053436.1988.10715302. 5

Isen, A.M. (2004). Positive affect and decision-making. In M. Lewis and J. Haviland-Jones (Eds.), *Handbook of Emotions*. New York: Guilford Press. 46

Jiang, T., Liu, F., and Chi, Y. (2015). Online information encountering: Modeling the process and influencing factors. *Journal of Documentation*, 71(6), 1135–1157. DOI: 10.1108/JD-07-2014-0100.

Jones, W. (2007). Personal information management. *Annual Review of Information Science and Technology*, 41, 453–504.DOI: 10.1002/aris.2007.1440410117. 48

Katz, E. (1959). Mass communications research and the study of popular culture: An editorial note on a possible future for this journal. Studies in Public Communication, 2, 1–6. Retrieved from http://repository.upenn.edu/asc_pa-pers/165. 5

Katz, E., Haas, H, and Gurevitch, M. (1973). On the use of the mass media for important things. *American Sociological Review*, 38(2), 164–181. DOI: 10.2307/2094393. 5

Kim, Y. (2012). Politics of representation in the digital media environment: Presentation of the female candidate between news coverage and the website in the 2007 Korean presidential primary. *Asian Journal of Communication*, 22, 601–620. DOI: 10.1080/01292986.2012.662513. 7

Kim, Y., Chen, H., and Zúñiga, H. (2013). Stumbling upon news on the Internet: Effects of incidental news exposure and relative entertainment use on political engagement. *Computers in Human Behavior*, 29, 2607–2614. DOI: 10.1016/j.chb.2013.06.005. 2, 7, 9, 10, 46, 56

Krugman, H.E. (1965). The impact of television advertising: Learning without involvement. *Public Opinion Quarterly*, 29, 349–356. DOI: 10.1086=267335. 8

Krugman, H.E. and Hartley, E.L. (1970). Passive learning from television. *Public Opinion Quarterly*, 34, 184–190. DOI: 10.1086=267788. 8

LaRose, Robert. (2010). The problem of media habits. *Communication Theory*, 20, 194–222. DOI: 10.1111/j.1468-2885.2010.01360.x. 6

Lee J.K. (2007). The effect of the Internet on homogeneity of the media agenda: A test of the fragmentation thesis. *Journalism and Mass Communication Quarterly*, 84(4), 745–760. DOI: 10.1177/107769900708400406. 7

Levy, M. R. and Windahl, S. (1984). Audience activity and gratifications: A conceptual clarification and exploration. *Communication Research*, 11, 51–78. DOI: 10.1177/009365084011001003. 6

Lincoln, Y.S. and Guba, E.G. (1985). *Naturalistic Inquiry*. Beverly Hills, CA: Sage Publications. 17

Makri, S. and Warwick, C. (2010). Information for inspiration: Understanding architects' information seeking and use behaviors to inform design. *Journal of the American Society for Information Science and Technology*, 61(9), 1745–1770. DOI: 10.1002/asi.21338. 11

Makri, S. and Blandford, A. (2012a). Coming across information serendipitously— Part 1: A process model. *Journal of Documentation*, 68(5), 684–705. 11, 45

Makri, S. and Blandford, A. (2012b). Coming across information serendipitously—Part 2: A classification framework. *Journal of Documentation*, 68(5), 706–724. DOI: 10.1108/00220411211256049. 3, 11, 46

McBirnie, A. (2008). Seeking serendipity: the paradox of control. *Aslib Proceedings*, 60(6), 600-618. DOI: 10.1108/00012530810924294. 11, 46

McQuail, D., Blumler, J.G., and Brown, J.R. (1972). The television audience: A revised perspective. In D. McQuail (Ed.), *Sociology of Mass Communications* (pp. 135–165): Harmondsworth, England: Penguin. 5

Mitchell, A., Kiley, J., Gottfried, J., and Guskin, E. (2013). *The Role of News on Facebook*. Pew Research Journalism Project. Retrieved January 24, 2016, from http://www.journalism.org/2013/10/24/the-role-of-news-on-facebook/. 7, 52, 56

Mitchelstein, E. and Boczkowski, P.J. (2010). Online news consumption research: An assessment of past work and an agenda for the future. *New Media and Society*, 12(7), 1085–1102. DOI: 10.1177/1461444809350193. 7, 55

Mutz, D.C. (2006). *Hearing the Other Side: Deliberative Versus Participatory Democracy*. New York: Cambridge University Press. DOI: 10.1017/CBO9780511617201. 2, 52

Nahl, D. (1998). Ethnography of novices' first use of web search engines: Affective control in cognitive processing. *Internet Reference Services Quarterly*, 3(2), 579–594. DOI: 10.1300/J136v03n02_09. 49

Nahl, D. (2005). Affective Load. In F. Karen E, S. Erdelez, and L. McKehnie (Eds.), *Information Theories* (pp. 39-44). Medford, NJ: Information Today Inc. 11

Nahl, D. and Bilal, D. (2007). *Information and Emotion: The Emergent Affective Paradigm in Information Behavior Research and Theory*. Medford, N.J: Information Today. 49

Nielsen, J. (1993). *Usability Engineering*. Boston: Academic Press. 18, 19

Nikolov, D., Oliveira, D.F.M., Flammini, A., and Menczer, F. (2015). Measuring online social bubbles. *PeerJ Computer Science*, 1(e38). DOI: 10.7717/peerj-cs.38. 52, 56

Nguyen, A. (2008). The contribution of online news attributes to its diffusion: An empirical exploration based on a proposed theoretical model for the micro-process of online news adoption/use. *First Monday*, 13(4), 1–24. DOI: 10.5210/fm.v13i4.2127. 7

Pálsdóttir, A. (2009). The connection between purposive information seeking and information encountering: A study of Icelanders' health and lifestyle information seeking. *Journal of Documentation*, 66(2), 224–244. DOI: 10.1108/00220411011023634. 11

Park, R.E. (1940). News as a Form of Knowledge: A Chapter in the Sociology of Knowledge. *American Journal of Sociology*, 45(5), 669–686. DOI: 10.1086/218445. xv

Pariser, E. (2011). *The Filter Bubble: What the Internet is Hiding from You*. New York: Penguin Press. 1, 51

Patton, M.Q. (2002). *Qualitative Research and Evaluation Methods* (3 ed.). Thousand Oaks, CA: Sage Publications. 17

Pentina, I. and Tarafdar, M. (2014). From "information" to "knowing": Exploring the role of social media in contemporary news consumption. *Computers in Human Behavior*, 35, 211–233. DOI: 10.1016/j.chb.2014.02.045. 43, 45, 52, 56

Peters, C. (2015). Introduction. Journalism Studies, 16(1), 1–11. DOI: 10.1080/1461670X.2014.889944. 5, 6

Prior, M. (2005). News vs. entertainment: How increasing media choice widen gaps in political knowledge. *American Journal of Political Science*, 49(3), 577–592. DOI: 10.1111/j.1540-5907.2005.00143.x. 7, 52

Purcell, K., Raine, L., Mitchell, A., Rosenstiel, T., and Olmstead, K. (2010). Understanding the participatory news consumer: How Internet and cell phone users have turned news into a social experience. *Pew Internet and American Life Project*. Retrieved April 30, 2010, from http://www.pewinternet.org/Reports/2010/Online-News.aspx. 2, 7, 8

Putnam, R.D. (1995). Bowling alone: America's declining social capital. *Journal of Democracy*, 6(1), 65–78. DOI: 10.1353/jod.1995.0002. 7

Putnam, R.D. (2000). *Bowling Alone: The Collapse and Revival of American Community*. New York: Simon and Schuster. DOI: 10.1145/358916.361990. 7

Ross, C.S. (1999). Finding without seeking: The information encounter in the context of reading for pleasure. *Information Processing and Management*, 35(6), 783–799. DOI: 10.1016/S0306-4573(99)00026-6. 11

Rubin, A.M. (1984). Ritualized and instrumental television viewing. *Journal of Communication*, 34(3), 67–77. DOI: 10.1111/j.1460-2466.1984.tb02174.x. 6

Rubin, V.L., Burkel, J., and Quan-Haase, A. (2011). Facets of serendipity in everyday chance encounters: A grounded theory approach to blog analysis. *Information Research*, 16(3), paper 488. Available at http://InformationR.net/ir/16-3/paper488.html. 11, 43, 46, 49

Salwen, M., Garrison, B., and Driscoll, P. (2005). The baseline survey projects: Exploring questions. In M. Salwen, B. Garrison and P. Driscoll (Eds.), *Online News and Public* (pp. 121–145). Mahwah: NJ: Lawrence Erlbaum. 2, 7, 9

Savolainen, R. (1995). Everyday life information seeking: Approaching information seeking in the context of "way of life." *Library and Information Science Research*, 17(3), 259–294. DOI: 10.1016/0740-8188(95)90048-9. 2, 15

Savolainen, R. (2007). Information behavior and information practice: Reviewing the "Umbrella Concepts" of information-seeking studies. *The Library Quarterly*, 77(2), 109–132. DOI: 10.1086/517840. 10

Scheufele, D.A. and Nisbet, M C. (2002). Being a citizen online: New opportunities and dead ends. *Harvard International Journal of Press/Politics*, 7(3), 55–75. DOI: 10.1177/1081180X0200700304. 7, 52

Severin, W. J. and Tankard, J.W. (2001). *Communication Theories: Origins, Methods, and Uses in the Mass Media*. New York: Longman. 6

Shim, M., Kelly, B., and Hornik, R. (2006). Cancer information scanning and seeking behavior is associated with knowledge, lifestyle choices, and screening. *Journal of Health Communication: International Perspectives*, 11(1 supp 1), 157–172. DOI: 10.1080/10810730600637475.

Smith, J. A. (2008). Beyond the Four Theories of the Press: A New Model for the Asian and the World Press. *Journalism and Communication Monographs*, 10(1), 4-63.

Siebert, F.S., Peterson, T., and Schramm, W. (1963). *Four Theories of the Press*. Urbana and Chicago: University of Illinois Press. 55

Strauss, A.L. and Corbin, J.M. (1998). *Basics of Qualitative Research: Techniques and Procedures for Developing Grounded Theory* (2nd ed.). Thousand Oaks, CA: Sage Publications. 20

Sun, X., Sharples, S., and Makri, S. (2011). A user-centered mobile diary study approach to understanding serendipity in information research. *Information Research*, 16(3), paper 492. Available at http://InformationR.net/ir/16-3/paper492.html. 11

Sunstein, C. (2001). *Republic.com*. Princeton, NJ: Princeton University Press. 1, 7

Sunstein, C. R. (2002). The law of group polarization. *The Journal of Political Philosophy*, 10(2), 175–195. DOI: 10.1111/1467-9760.00148.

Tian, Y. and Robinson, J. D. (2009). Incidental health information use on the internet. *Health Communication*, 24(1), 41–49. DOI: 10.1080/10410230802606984. 10

Tewksbury, D., Weaver, A.J., and Maddex, B.D. (2001). Accidentally informed: Incidental news exposure on the World Wide Web. *Journalism and Mass Communication Quarterly*, 78(3), 533. DOI: 10.1177/107769900107800309. 1, 2, 7, 8, 10

Thorson, K. and Wells, C. (2015). Curated flows: A framework for mapping media exposure in the digital age. *Communications Theory*, 1–20. 51

Toms, E.G. (2000). Understanding and facilitating the browsing of electronic text. *International Journal of Human-Computer Studies*, 52, 423–452. DOI: 10.1006/ijhc.1999.0345. 11

Trilling, D. and Schoenbach, K. (2012). Skipping current affairs: The non-users of online and offline news. *European Journal of Communication*, 28(1), 35–51. DOI: 10.1177/0267323112453671. 1

Tufekci, Z. (2014). Engineering the public: Big data, surveillance, and computational politics. *First Monday*, 19(7). DOI: 10.5210/fm.v19i7.4901. 51

Urquhart, C., Light, A., Thomas, R., Barker, A., Yeoman, A., Cooper, J., et al. (2003). Critical incident technique and explication interviewing in studies of information behavior. *Library and Information Science Research*, 25(1), 63–88. DOI: 10.1016/S0740-8188(02)00166-4. 18

Vermersch, P. (1994). *L' Entretien d 'Explicitation*. Paris: ESF. 19

Whittaker, S. (2011). Personal information management: from information consumption to curation. *Annual Review of Information Science and Technology*, 45, 3–62. DOI: 10.1002/aris.2011.1440450108. 48

Williamson, K. (1998). Discovered by chance: The role of incidental information acquisition in an ecological model of information use. *Library and Information Science Research*, 20(1), 23–40. DOI: 10.1016/S0740-8188(98)90004-4. 11

Windahl, S. (1981). Uses and gratifications at the crossroads. *Mass Communication Review Yearbook*, 2, 174–185. 6

Yadamsuren, B. (2013). Potential of Inducing Serendipitous News Discovery in a Social Gaming Environment. *Proceedings of the American Society for Information Science and Technology* (ASIS&T), 50(1), 1–4. DOI: 10.1002/meet.14505001157. 56

Yadamsuren, B. and Heinström, J. (2011). Emotional reactions to incidental exposure to online news. Information Research, 16(3), paper 486. Available at http://InformationR.net/ir/16-3/paper486.html. 30, 46, 60

Yin, J. (2008). Beyond the Four Theories of the Press: A New Model for the Asian & the World Press. *Journalism and Mass Communication Monographs*, 10(1), 3-62. DOI: 10.1177/152263790801000101. 55

Yuan, E. (2011). News consumption across multiple media platforms: A repertoire approach. *Information, Communication and Society*, 14(7), 998–1016. DOI: 10.1080/1369118X.2010.549235. 6

Zillmann, D., Chen, L., Knobloch-Westerwick, S., and Callison, C. (2004). Effects of lead framing on selective exposure to internet news reports. *Communication Research*, 31(1), 58–81. DOI: 10.1177/0093650203260201. 7

Zuckerman, E. (2013). *Rewire: Digital Cosmopolitans in the Age of Connection*. New York: W.W. Norton and Company. 1, 2

Zukin, C. and Snyder, R. (1984). Passive learning: When the media environment is the message. *Public Opinion Quarterly*, 48(3), 629–638. DOI: 10.1086/268864. 8

# Author Biographies

**Dr. Borchuluun Yadamsuren** is an instructor at Columbia College in Columbia Missouri. Her research focuses on the information behavior of news consumers, serendipitous information discovery, gaming, and human computer interaction. As a part of her postdoctoral fellowship at the Reynolds Journalism Institute, she created the *MU Tiger Challenge* social game to expose college students to news via serendipitous discovery. With the project, she conducted an experimental study to induce serendipity in social game environment. This game project was highlighted in the book *Digital Innovations for Mass Communications: Engaging the User*. Yadamsuren received her Ph.D. in information science and M.A. in journalism from the University of Missouri. She earned her M.S. in computer science from the Mongolian Technical University and B.S. in computer science from the Novosibirsk State Technical University in Russia.

**Dr. Sanda Erdelez** (@iesanda) is a Professor at the University of Missouri iSchool (School of Information Science and Learning Technologies) in Columbia, Missouri, where she is also the founding director of the MU Information Experience Laboratory. She received her LL.B. and LL.M from the University of Osijek Law School in Croatia and a Ph.D. in information transfer from Syracuse University. Her research interests include human information behavior, human-computer interaction, and usability evaluation in online environments. She has been internationally recognized for her pioneering research of information encountering. She is the co-editor of *Theories of Information*, a classic reading in human information behavior research and the author of numerous peer reviewed articles. Dr. Erdelez received the 2015 Award for Outstanding Contribution to Information Behavior Research from the Association for Information Science and Technology (ASIS&T) SIG USE and was inducted into the SIG USE Academy of Fellows.